Wawewa Mepemoa

Jacqueline H. Day

BY

jd daniels

SAVVY PRESS
NEW YORK

The Old Wolf Lady
Wawewa Mepemoa
Jacqueline H. Day

Second Edition
Copyright @ 2014 jd daniels

Photographs reprinted by permission
of Jacqueline H. Day
Cover Art by Peg Cullen

ISBN: 978-1-939113-15-3
Library of Congress Control Number:
2014938633

First Edition Sponsored by Grants
from the Iowa Arts Council & Kirkwood
Community College

Includes bibliographical references.
Printed in the United States of America
Worldwide Distribution

Jacqueline H. Day
1918-2002

What is life?
It is the flash of a firefly in the night.
It is the breath of a buffalo in the wintertime.
It is the little shadow which runs across
the grass and loses itself in the sunset.

Crowfoot, Blackfoot Warrior and Orator, 1830–1890

For My Family and the Seekers in the World

PREFACE

And while I stood there
I saw more than I can tell,
and I understood more than I saw;
for I was seeing in a sacred manner
the shapes of things in the spirit,
and the shape of all shapes as they must
live together like one being.

Black Elk, *Black Elk Speaks*

The decision to publish a second edition of the life story of my Aunt Jacqueline H. Day was a big one. For the research process, time was my enemy. I had attempted to get the book out before Jackie passed and to this end, rushed the final stages of the original biography's evolution. Unfortunately, even with that, *The Old Wolf Lady* wasn't in print before Jackie left this world.

Jackie gave me photographs to use, but they were not included in the first version. Many readers have expressed a desire to see them. I was also aware that she would have loved more of a connection made with her Native American ancestry and her husband's family.

And so I present *The Old Wolf Lady, Wawewa Mepemoa,* with photographs, favored Native American sayings, and further history on her husband's family.

Enjoy.

∾

Assertiveness was a key characteristic of Jacqueline H. Day, and I was continually reminded of this during the years this book evolved. I was brought up to believe that assertive/aggressive women were something to be frowned at—to be given derogatory names; certainly they were not women to emulate.

I didn't know Jackie Day during my formative years. If I had, my enlightenment may have come much earlier. The story you will read here is about a woman raised in poverty who overcame great odds and refused to say "yes" to a society that tried to reshape her.

As an adult, Jackie Day did not like how Iowans wanted to ignore the soldier's plight in Vietnam, nor how they were treated when they came home. What did she do? She went to the battlefield. Then she came home and spread the word—Jackie Day style. Jackie Day did not like how women were not getting the recognition they deserved for their work. What did she do? She acted—Jackie Day style. Jackie Day did not like how African Americans were being treated in the 60s. What did she do? She acted Jackie Day style. Jackie Day learned that the Native Americans in Tama, Iowa, wanted more recognition. What did she do? She acted. That's who Jackie Day was—an assertive woman of action—through and through. During her lifetime, her electric energy reached out, found and encouraged the best in others.

While still living she was rewarded for her work by being inducted into both the East High Hall of Fame and into the Iowa Women's Hall of Fame. Shelter houses and means of transportation have been named after her. A brick was laid in the Plaza of Heroines at Iowa State University in Ames. At the reservation in Tama, Iowa, she was adopted into the Wolf Tribe and given a name that transcribes to *The Old Wolf Lady*. Jackie Day died on June 23, 2002, knowing that her work had not gone unnoticed.

Jackie Day was a Republican who was often in the public eye. Even before she could vote, politics played a major role in her life.

However, for those politically minded readers who may not want to read this book because they are not Republican, I would like to say that this book is not in any way backing the Republican Party, or any party for that matter. This biography honors a woman who was first and foremost a humanist.

This is a story about a woman who took her life journey very seriously, one who gave to others more than she took. Hers was a life of strife and triumph, of human dignity—a testament to human-hood. The process of writing this book came, with doubts and trepidation.

I had been looking for my next writing project when I heard Jackie Day (at my older brother's retirement party) telling my sister a humorous anecdote. Her storytelling abilities made me stop in my tracks and listen. Shortly after that I spoke to my mother and asked her to remind me what Aunt Jackie had done with her life. Somewhere back in my memory I remembered she had done something, but what?

My mother said she had been in politics and was often featured in the newspaper, but she didn't know much more than that. I was curious. What had she done? I asked some more questions to other family members. Yes, she's had an incredible life.

"You should call her," my brother said. "Her great grandmother was a Sioux, you know."

No, I didn't know.

I'm not a telephone type of person; we had a wall phone when we lived on the orchard where I was raised. Three shorts and a long was our ring. Having to stand in our three-bedroom farmhouse in order to talk and having no privacy (any neighbor could pick up the line while you were talking), I never developed the habit of feeling comfortable on the phone. To this day, I am still amazed when I hear a friend chatting with another person or family member on their phones for half an hour; the whole act seems alien to me. I wrote Jackie instead. She wrote me back and said she was interested.

I went to her apartment the following week.

When I saw her résumé, my right eyebrow arched in the shape of a sleeping comma. This woman should have her story told. No doubt about it. But why by me? Almost immediately my motivation plummeted to below sea level. How in the world had I thought I would want to research and write the life history of another person? I experienced a panic attack created by a sense of obligation I wasn't sure I could meet. Immediately, I slipped into a state of avoidance.

Time passed. My motivation was nonexistent and I knew I had to face Jackie. Darn. More time passed. My guilt mounted. Finally, one day after visiting my brother, I stopped by Luther Park where Aunt Jackie lived (she had spent the day with her son and his family at their home in Des Moines) to tell her that I didn't think I could tackle the project. I explained that I was a creative writer who needed a sense of freedom in her writing and that I had past baggage that made me fearful of commitment. I assured her I had made a mistake in proposing to write her biography. She should find someone else. To my dismay, Aunt Jackie knew just what to do.

Jackie seated me in her living room and then left with the aid of a walker. I looked about her room at the Native American Mandela, the dream catcher, and multiple photographs of her children and husband I gazed at the dream catcher knowing that the myth is that they catch the bad dreams and let the good dreams go through. I wondered what Jackie's bad dreams were.

I saw a motion out of the corner of my eye. A starling landed on the railing of the small balcony off the living room. Its wings billowed then pulled in to hug its body. It seemed comfortable, at peace, much like Jackie.

Maybe the dream catcher and the meditative power of the Mandela worked.

Or was it the peace she felt from her Christian faith?

Or was it both?

Or none of these things?

Jackie returned with a *Sunday Des Moines Register* news clipping in her hands. "Here, read this. It was published over twenty-five years ago," she said.

I smiled, taking in her silver hair, her large beaded earrings, her colorful long caftan, then lowered my eyes and read the words of Robert Hullihan, a reporter now deceased: "Bejeweled and exotically perfumed like a woman lately come from the throne room of a fanciful kingdom, Mrs.

Jacqueline Day sat on the lawn behind Veterans Hospital, looking down with distaste into a cup of spinach..."

I grinned and scanned the page.

She was fifty-seven at the time of the writing. I looked at the now eighty-two-year-old woman and read on.

"I hate it," said the woman of imperial costume, referring to the spinach. "It's a hang-up from my childhood. We were so poor that I slept in a bathtub the first four years of my life. My father was a garbage man. He was a drunk before drunks were popular."

Spunky language. Straight shooter. No hiding behind.

I knew right then that I liked this woman, this stranger who was my aunt. Yes, it would be a challenge and a commitment to take on this project, but I liked a challenge. No doubt about that. Here was a strong, dynamic woman. I was intrigued.

Yet, was she too strong? Would she want a control over my writing that I couldn't give?

"Well..." I said, still hesitant.

And then I told her a little more about me, about my philosophy of writing, how it had always been important for me to be in charge of my work. That I was a poet and fiction writer, who had never written a biography. I had never published a book, and I didn't want to disappoint her.

"You know, Jackie, when I was married, I spent hours sewing clothes, cooking, entertaining, and then I did crafts, all this while raising children, now I spend my time writing. I like it.

"The truth is, writing feeds my soul. I'm drawn to it like a meteor to the earth. I make most of my choices of how I'll spend my time because of it.

"It's while writing that I feel my greatest sense of freedom. I protect my writing, my sense of white space. I can never allow these aspects of my writing to disappear. I don't want my writing to be a chore. I want it to be a friend, a good friend, one you look forward to going home to, look forward to smiling at over your first cup of coffee, that sort of thing. That's why I keep doing this. It's my passion."

She listened and then looked directly into my eyes: "You can make my story fiction if you want to. You're the writer, not me. You'll have full artistic license. You can use any photos you wish. More than one person has proposed writing my story, you know, but it's a matter of who you want to spend your time with."

That was the clincher. Sitting in a room with a Native American Mandela and doll with her hand resting on the head of a wolf, I felt release from my sense of being strangled. My journey with the Old Wolf Lady from the East Side of Des Moines began.

How did life begin for this woman? Who were the people who helped shape her destiny? What particular Iowa soil was squeezed between her toes? What was happening in history as this child grew to become a woman? How did she react to her personal experience? What made her tick? What will history say about Jacqueline H. Day? These were just some of the questions I needed to answer.

After serious thought concerning the political correctness issue of how to address Jackie Day in this text, for two reasons, I decided not to use today's accepted last name reference for women. For those readers who don't understand what I am referring to: It is taught that referring to men in a text by their last names shows respect. It is thought that referring to women in nonfiction by the first names is demeaning. Thus, writers, aware of this issue, have consistently and pointedly, out of respect for their female subject, referred to women in the same manner as men. In most cases I agree with this rationale. Women need, in all areas, to be placed on the same level of respect as men. But this case is different. First, use of "Day" often caused confusion in a sentence. Second, and more important, in conversations with Jackie Day, she explicitly expressed that she wanted her story told in a personal, down-home way. She liked being called Jackie. If anyone didn't respect her for that reason, that was their problem.

"Color me human," she said with a chuckle.

TABLE OF

CONTENTS

When you know who you are; when your mission is clear and you burn with the inner fire of unbreakable will; no cold can touch your heart; no deluge can dampen your purpose. You know that you are alive.

~ Chief Seattle, Duwamish (1780–1866)

1

Nurtured in a Bathtub

*I do not think the measure of a civilization
is how tall its buildings of concrete are,
but rather how well its people have learned to relate
to their environment and fellow man*

~ Sun Bear of the Chippewa Tribe

"Hello, Grandma." The Hispanic waiter touched Jackie's shoulder. "How are you?"

I smiled. So it was each time we· entered a new environment, Jacqueline H. Day, a woman with an electric personality, was known, respected, and loved. That was obvious. It became a personal pleasure to me, her niece, to see the warmth that was extended to this woman who had been married to my deceased uncle just three months short of fifty years. And so the journey of discovery began…

Jacqueline H. Armstrong was born to Mary Jane Reeves and Louis David Armstrong in 1918 in Des Moines, Iowa, two years before the Nineteenth Amendment was ratified guaranteeing American women citizens the right to vote. This was the same year Mary Sanger won her suit in New

York allowing doctors to advise their married patients about birth control for health purposes. Approximately one hundred and thirty years earlier, a Native American Shoshone woman, Sacagawea, with her infant child, served as a pivotal translator for the Lewis and Clark Expedition.

Although not treated as equals, women have always been an integral part of change in America and Jackie H. Armstrong would gradually show that, like Sanger and Sacagawea, she wished to be an active participant for change.

Her mother, Mary Jane, was a short, stout, plain woman who never wore makeup. When she worked in the yard, a headscarf was tied under her chin and her cotton housedress was made out of feed sacks. When Mary Jane went to church, she wore her one good dress and a hat with a netted veil that covered her forehead. She killed, dressed, and cooked chickens for supper. Baked her own bread. Washed clothes in a tub of boiling water with homemade soap she had made. Scrubbed clothes on a scrub board and hung them out to dry. Cooked and served three meals a day, only sitting when everyone else had their plates full.

She had few words for her children and did not talk back when her husband, Louis, got drunk and violent. She had little grass in her yard and few flowers. Her house had never been painted and the curtains at her windows were plastic. When a window broke, she fixed it with a strip of masking tape. She had no method of birth control, raised her children with no help from her husband, and didn't go to bed without getting down on her hands and knees and scrubbing her kitchen floor. She had no washing machine, no dishwasher, no electric iron, no refrigerator (only an icebox), no TV, and electric lights only in the living room and kitchen. With little education and six kids, she had few choices. She was an uncommonly patient, benevolent, unselfish person who was forty when she gave birth at home to Jackie.

Mary Jane was one tough, amazing woman.

Jackie's sister Edna was eight when Jackie was born. Her other sisters, Elna, Marie, and Opal were married, as was her only brother, Charlie. The family lived in the lowlands in East Des Moines—in an area called the Southeast Bottoms. During the depression, fifteen family members of the Armstrong family lived together under one roof. The only one working full-time outside of the home was Jackie's illiterate father who worked in the coal mines at $2.50 per day.

Jackie's bed was a bathtub with a quilt folded in the bottom. The family didn't have indoor plumbing, but they did own the bathtub. It was to be Jackie's bed until she was over four years old.

Although the house was crowded, Mary Jane took in boarders during the days of the Iowa State Fair. Her children worked at the food stands. Their front yard became a parking lot, providing more income. Were these bad memories? Nah. It was a blast. Not only was the yearly fair full of laughter and new faces—it was extra income, sorely needed. Jackie said they felt lucky. Charmed. Special.

Jackie believed her youthful experience of being part of the excitement of the August days where colorful Ferris wheels whirled, music filtered through the air, crowds of people brought their prized garden produce, animals, crafts, and baked goods for display, cemented her lifelong love for the festivities of the fair.

Perhaps her paternal great grandmother, a full-blooded Oglala Sioux, hauled a prized pumpkin to the fair. Jackie said she was a truck gardener who supported her husband, Jackie's great grandfather, when he would sit under a tree on lazy Iowa days and read voraciously before going to the college classroom to teach. Was Jackie's great grandfather really a college professor? Jackie believed so, but I have been unable to verify that it was a fact. Jackie said the family thought their great grandfather was lazy (after all, all he did was read and talk to students all day).

3

Jackie said she admired their hard-working great grandmother. This was not an unusual stance for a working family. Jackie, however, admired her because she was Sioux.

Jackie often described her father as "a drunk before drunks were popular." She remembered once that he made a rather large quantity of grape wine and drank it all in two days. His loud words far overshadowed the quiet, soft demeanor of his wife, Mary Jane, a religious person who raised her children to respect their elders.

Mary Jane's mother was of a different ilk. She came to dislike not only Jackie's father, Louis, for his drunken ways, her hatred spread to his children as well. Jackie remembered passing Grandma Reeve's home more than four times a day going from school to home, to the store, but never thinking of stopping to have milk and cookies or a friendly chat with the woman who was her grandmother.

At home Mary Jane sat at the cook stove, humming religious hymns, apparently resigned to the life with the man she had chosen for her husband. Only for one short period did Jackie recall her mother working outside the home, and that was to clean an office building, more than likely while her father was recovering from a mining accident that changed his life forever. Back pain. Increased drinking. Heightened violent episodes. Dark times.

When I look at the pictures of Jackie's parents, I can't help but think of the characters in John Steinbeck's *Grapes of Wrath*. Like Steinbeck's characters, the Days were honest, hard-working people struggling to make ends meet in a land that had promised riches.

It's not that surprising that many Americans turned to alcohol to mask their disappointment in the American Dream that they knew would never be part of their reality.

Louis Armstrong worked as a coal miner in south Des Moines, but one hot day the ceiling of the mine collapsed and under the rubble Louis's spine was badly injured. After his recovery, he worked at a cement plant for some time, and then went to work as a garbage collector for the city of Des Moines. After work and on the weekends, loud, raw language rang through the tiny, thin-walled, unpainted house. The home brew became stronger.

Jackie remembered being embarrassed to tell her friends what her father really did, so she made up her own story. He was a "G Man," she told everyone—a term that held sufficient romantic intrigue to satisfy her own active imagination while hiding her embarrassment.

For two decades, Louis Armstrong worked as a garbage man. For his entire life he drank too much, raving in the home where the intelligent Jackie devoured hungrily any book he retrieved from the garbage cans, while her mother hummed to quiet tunes of salvation near the stove.

When Jackie contracted smallpox, her mother diagnosed her problem as the "itch" and scrubbed her with lye soap. She continued to go to school. No doctor was ever brought to the home. The school nurse finally diagnosed the illness, but not before everyone in the family came down with the illness, including her sister-in-law's baby, born during the eventual quarantine.

Not long after that Jackie's mother contracted typhoid fever. In those days everything was treated at home and seeing her mother so ill and losing her hair, Jackie was understandably terrified.

According to Jackie her father's remedies were usually worse than the illness and, more often than not, were drastic and painful. Many of them he had learned from his Native American grandmother.

Jackie once had a spot on her arm he thought was ringworm. He took his pipe apart and smeared the pure nicotine on her arm. It went into her blood stream. She fainted. The end result worked similarly, she said, to the present-day nicotine patch. She never smoked. "There's a silver lining in all sow's purses," Jackie said, smoothing her

5

silk skirt. Well, that was one way to look at such abusive behavior.

Jackie didn't have her mother's personality. She took after her dad. Mary Armstrong was a gentle woman who never raised her voice. Jackie claimed her dad never lowered his. Every other word he spoke was a cuss word. He embellished his language with vulgarities, never saying, "Well, I'll be damned." Instead, "I'll be a jumping-up and down fiddler's dick." Jackie grew up thinking his way of talking was all a part of the English language. Her colorful adult persona always reflected this rich, funny, but raw way of putting words together—this style of speaking became a Jackie Day trademark. One I admired greatly, but could never pull off.

With older siblings who loved to make fun of her, and poorly informed parents who didn't understand illness and treatment, Jackie developed an inferiority complex, feeling, she said, as welcomed as "a bastard at a family reunion." When her sister Elna was dating, she'd point Jackie out to all the young men: "Look at the elephant ears on that kid." And, "Did you ever see such an ugly kid in your life?"

Comments like this affected her self-esteem, but Jackie Day did not become a silent, shy wallflower. On the contrary, she became a saucy teenager with a voice who fought for the underdog. Jackie created a strong, powerful shield that served her well.

Her dad may have been a drunk, but Jackie loved and defended him. Here's a perfect example:

One Sunday Jackie's Aunt Grace and Uncle Fred joined them for dinner after church. Aunt Grace shared in Jackie's grandmother's dislike for Jackie's dad.

"Do you have to eat with your elbows on the table?" she asked, tearing her roll in half.

The feisty young Jackie set down her fork. "How you feel about my dad doesn't keep *you* from putting your feet under his table, does it?"

"Go to your room! Don't ever talk to your aunt like that again," her mother said.

Shocked at her mother's words and her tone, Jackie looked to her dad for help. His solemn, red-rimmed eyes were downcast, his cap set at an angle on his head. His whiskers were peppered in gray. He would not look at her.

Livid, Jackie slid her chair out from the table and stomped out of the room.

This is the one time Jackie remembered the anger of her quiet mother being voiced—the only time. Pretty amazing considering the circumstances.

Understandably, the overworked Mary Jane had very little time to give her youngest child and did not voice her love. Consequently, Jackie felt unwanted. She spent a lot of time alone and played in the dark coal shed, hiding there at times when her older sister came for a visit.

Staring out of the cracks in the walls, she watched as her dad spit out harsh words to her mother and sister. Often, Jackie would hold a piece of coal in her hand and make a wish—a wish for family harmony—a wish that never came true.

The poverty of the family kept her from having a bike, a wagon, a doll, or a pet. She learned early to entertain herself with what she had. Leaves from bushes became food to be served to imaginary visitors. Patterns in the clouds provided adventures.

She crocheted doilies. And, of course, she loved to go to school.

School became a place where she made friends—where she could lose herself in her studies—where she was not told she was ugly.

"Look at that ugly creature," her sisters said. "Have you ever seen such a skinny kid? She has to have worms!"

"I've got just the medicine," her dad said, setting down his mug of beer, wiping off his grisly face, and heading for the unpainted clapboard house.

Time after time, her sister and dad "wormed" her with a foul-tasting, smelly patent medicine called Vermafuge. Jackie swallowed, imagining worms living in her body. "Kill them before they eat my heart," she begged.

Did the worms cause her fainting spells? Or did the medication? Or did the verbal attacks?

One thing is known, at the age of seventeen she was diagnosed with primary TB, a disease common among the poor.

When you look at Jackie's pictures, you see that she was a lovely little girl and a pretty teenager. Her hair was thick and black. She was slender and had long legs. She was smart. Were her older siblings jealous of the pretty, intelligent child?

When asked, Jackie said she didn't know. But she did believe that it was because of the way she was treated by them that she developed her fiercely independent attitude— an "I'll show you" stance to life.

At a very young age she decided to make the most of what she had. She would never let someone dictate what her life was going to be. She would be her own decision maker. Pain makes gain, remember?

Religion played a dynamic role in Jackie's upbringing. Her mother was a Methodist who rarely went to church. Her sister Elna joined the Catholic Church, to the horror of her mother who thought only Methodists would go to heaven. Her brother Charlie married a Catholic. Her older sister married a Jewish man. So, despite her parents' wishes, diversity was the key in the volatile Armstrong household.

As a young child, Jackie's mother dropped her off at a nearby church, The Free Methodist, a strict denomination of Methodist, who among other things, did not believe that the newspaper should be read on Sundays. The vulnerable, wide-eyed Jackie accepted God as her savior while she gathered fallen bird feathers in the yard and stuck them in bottles on a table.

One day she read about Kateri Tekakwitha, St. Kateri, a Native American woman born around 1656 of an Algonquin mother and a non-Christian Mohawk chief. As a young girl, like Jackie, Tekakwitha had smallpox. As an adult Tekakwitha lived a saintly life teaching and helping the sick. Jackie connected. She decided that she lived in an evil household. After all, her parents did not attend church regularly. Her father's drinking, she surmised, had to be an act of Satan. She vowed to atone for their heathen behavior. Consequently, as an adult, Jackie never drank alcohol or smoked and continued to attend church regularly until the day she died, but she drew the line at a life led as a nun and she had no desire to be known or be a "goody-two-shoes" as she called it—her love of slot machines and gambling was well known. Through the years her Christian beliefs intermingled with her own Native American spirituality.

There's a story Jackie loved to tell that her mother passed on to her. It goes like this: It seems the great grandmother mentioned earlier, an Oglala Sioux, supplemented her income by selling vegetables and nuts. One day, she took Jackie's mother into town to sell a buckboard load of hickory nuts. They stopped at a department store on the East Side and the great grandmother asked the merchant if he knew where she could sell some nuts. "I've got nuts in here. Know who might want some?"

Grinning, he gave her an address. When her great grandmother and young Mary Jane went to the door, they were greeted by a big woman in a red kimono. Her hair was carrot red and her fingernails were painted.

When her great grandmother asked the woman if she wanted some hickory nuts, the woman put both hands on her hips, tipped her head back and laughed. "Lady," she said. "We got more nuts than Country Club." To the audience's delight, she made sure to say the last line loud and clear.

Startled, her great grandmother suddenly realized where the man had sent her. Mortified, she grabbed Mary Jane's hand, turned and jumped down the steps three at a time, whipping the horse into a gallop all the way back to the department store. Hollering at the top of her lungs, she chased the merchant with the buggy whip. "You crappy-assed son of a bitch," the great grandmother screamed. Swat. Swat.

Jackie's mother loved telling the story to her children, but she always lowered her voice to a whisper when she said the last line.

As a child Jackie's family was so poor that the only concession to Christmas was her dad getting drunk and running around the house yelling, "On Donner, On Blitzen."

She never had a tree or lights or wrapped presents. But, she claimed, she never felt deprived. It was all she knew. Her friends were in the same situation. It was the depression, after all. She remembered one Christmas Eve with clarity.

"Here, girl, this is for you," her dad said in a gruff tone. Both of his hands were behind his back. "Pick one." Excited, she touched his left arm. He chuckled and slowly brought it around. She pulled the crumpled dress to her chest, hugging it close as if it were a delicate kitten. It was pink and the fact it was we know what to do with here.

As an adult, Jackie compensated for her childhood Christmas experiences. She attended church faithfully, was known as a generous giver of gifts, and a woman who loved everything about Christmas.

Jackie never forgot a frightening experience that happened when she was thirteen. She was staying for the summer with her sister Elna, who worked as a bookkeeper for Reeds Ice Cream in Omaha. This particular season, the sister had a ground floor apartment, and one day Elna was doing her laundry when she burned herself. She called the druggist to deliver some ointment, which he did. Jackie had to get into the cash box that Elna brought home every night to pay the delivery boy. When Jackie noticed the young man eyeing the box, she shut it quickly.

That night when Jackie and her sister were both lying under the sheet, a dark shadow crept to the bed. Thunder and lightning shattered the night sky. Their eyes popped open. The man had on a cap. Raindrops dripped off the bill. He tied them to the headboard with silk hose and began to put a gag into Elna's mouth. "Please, don't, I won't make a sound," she begged.

He hesitated and leaned closer. "Where's the box?"

Saying nothing, she shook her head.

"I said: Where's the damn money?"

Again, Elna remained silent.

The man dropped the gag and went to the other side of the bed. He sat and put his hand on Jackie's shoulder.

"Stop! Don't touch her. I'll tell you. Stop!"

Minutes later, the man left. Jackie wiggled her hands free, and then untied her sister. They called the police.

For weeks after, they slept with rows of glass milk bottles encircling their bed.

Scanning police photos never produced a suspect.

At thirteen Jackie learned that even inside your home you are not safe from possible harm. She learned at an early age to take measures for self-protection, knowledge that would come in handy in her adult life.

Jackie's mother

Chicken killin' day

Jackie's dad, Louis Armstrong, and
Mary Jane, her mother

2

Ah…Love

All over the earth the faces of living things are all alike.
Look upon these faces of children without number and with
children in their arms that they may face the winds and
walk the good road to the day of quiet.

~ Black Elk

In junior high Jackie met Harold Day, a teenager two grades ahead of her. He was handsome, quiet and industrious. She was pretty and intelligent.

"Hey, Jack, you want to go for a soda?"

"Well, I don't know. I've got to study."

"Ah, come on, want a float?"

Their instant attraction was mutual. Soon they became sweethearts. Often they walked to school together.

"I heard you were in a contest."

"Where'd ya hear that?" she asked.

"Oh, around." He kicked a stone.

"Yeah, well, it was at the fairgrounds."

"You win or anything?" His eyes sparkled.

She rolled her eyes. "Hardly."

"Oh. Well, you should have."

Her eyebrows shot up. "Not in a bathing suit."

14

His eyes shot to her ankles and then slowly raised. "Hell, I bet you looked like a million bucks in a bathing suit. Look at those legs."

"Well, it felt funny—being up there in front of all those people. I quit."

He shrugged. "Their bad luck."

She smiled and took his arm. "My girlfriends think I'm bossy. You might not like to be with me very long."

"I could use a good boss." He placed his hand over hers. "Yeah?"

"Yeah. The guys think you're something you know."

She stopped short. "Why?"

"They say you're going to do something with your life."

"They do?"

They stepped forward.

"That's what they say."

"And what do *you* say?" She swiped her long hair off her shoulders.

"I think you're one smart looker, for a girl named Jack."

Jackie laughed. She liked the nickname of "Jack." She liked this handsome young man who went by "Skip."

During her early high school years, Jackie's older sister Edna plucked her bushy eyebrows, taught her some make-up tricks and bought her the first new clothes and shoes she had ever had.

Comfort level and confidence rising, Jackie became more active in extracurricular activities.

She participated in more than in previous years.

In the midst of the depression in 1936 Skip graduated from high school, joined the Navy, and left for California. Jackie became an avid letter writer and remained true to their relationship. While Harold was absent, a devastating family tragedy that happened to her brother-in-law became a pivotal event in Jackie's young life.

It all happened at The Silver Dollar Bar in East Des Moines.

It was a steamy August Sunday afternoon. The bar was closed, but the door was standing open to let in a breeze that sifted down the street.

Don (named changed) was wiping off the bar. He turned when he heard footsteps.

"Hey, you, creep, you been with my wife?"

Don's eyes narrowed.

"I'm talking to you," the intruder growled.

"I don't have anything to say to you."

In a quick step the man was at the edge of the bar before Don could get out of the way, the man had the front of his shirt crumbled in his hand.

"You stay away from my wife!"

Don reached under the bar. The explosion that came from the revolver in his hand took off the man's face.

Don received a life sentence. Edna was incensed at the injustice. She and Jackie campaigned for fourteen years to get him released. Finally they were successful.

"Hey, Jack, guess what? He went back to that guy's wife."

"Figures."

"Yeah, it figures."

When Jackie's dad's job was threatened, she and her sister went door to door passing out flyers to make sure the right councilman was elected so her dad's job would be secure. Jackie figured the work she did to get her brother-in-law released from prison and the work she and her sister did to help her dad were the catalysts for her later interest in politics. Writing all the letters was fascinating. Being successful in accomplishing their goal was rewarding. Going door-to-door was fun. The grass-root seed was planted.

While in high school, Jackie earned her lunches by working in a nearby tearoom and she wrote a humor column for the school paper. True to her "smart aleck" attitude to life, she had become the humor columnist after she criticized the column and the teacher in charge threw out a challenge: "So, if you don't think it's written well, write it yourself." She took the job.

She was also a member of the National Honor Society, a senior class officer, and a member of the Toastmistress Club. It's easy to see why her classmates thought she was going to do something with her life.

When she was a senior, she was offered a scholarship at Drake University, but like most scholarships, it did not cover all expenses. She turned down the offer. Her family needed an indoor toilet and help with the cost of groceries. It was a tough decision. When she found out that she could get a job at Bankers Life (a hard to get job for a young woman in this time), she interviewed and soon began to bring home fifteen dollars a week.

The year was 1936, a landmark year for women in America. The United States Supreme Court declassified birth control information as obscene. Contraceptive devices could finally be imported to the United States, and Margaret Mead's *Sex and Temperament in Three Primitive Societies* that challenged sex-role assumptions was the popular book of the day for intelligent, avid readers like Jackie Day.

It was a big year for Jackie Day as well. By turning down the Drake Scholarship, she gave up her chances of receiving a college education—a choice that may have affected just how far up the ladder toward the glass ceiling this determined young woman of note would climb.

That same year she made a home improvement loan and had a bathroom put in the family house where she still lived. Her dad, however, would only go to the outhouse.

One time her mother asked Louis, "Why do you still go to that outside toilet now that we have a bathroom in the house?"

"Well, I'll tell you something, Mary," he said. "It never did seem sanitary to me to take a crap in the house."

In later years, whenever Jackie cleaned a toilet, and she

17

said she cleaned a "hell of a lot of them" during her lifetime, she remembered his comment and laughed.

"My dad wasn't," she said, "that far wrong on that issue."

Jackie in her volunteer uniform

Skip 1936

In California

3

The Journey

With temptation comes, I don't say, "Yes," and I don't say, "No." I say, "Later."

~ Dr. A.C. Ross (Ehanamani), Lakota

During the two years Jackie worked for Bankers Life and lived at home, she and Harold wrote continually to each other declaring their love. Their relationship flourished as they slowly learned more about each other's thoughts and dreams.

"What's your biggest fantasy, Jack?"

"Having my own office."

"Ah, what would you do with an office? Women don't have offices."

"I'd work in it, of course."

"What about you, Skip? What's your fantasy?"

"Having babies with you."

"Oh, Skip!"

Eventually, he proposed and asked her to come to the West Coast and marry. She was in love. Of course, she would marry—that's what women did. Would her fantasy of having her own office evaporate?

Would she become the woman she dreamed of being?

In 1938, two years after she graduated from high school, Jackie Armstrong climbed onto a bus and traveled to Hollywood, California, to marry the handsome, quiet Harold Day. Two of her friends from Des Moines accompanied her to be bridesmaids. Three days after the wedding Harold was sent to Alaska for duty for six weeks. His salary was $54 a month. Their apartment rent was $25 a month. The young bride, her friends now returned to Des Moines, spent long lonely days on the beach, spending little, but thinking often of the man she loved who would soon return to her—her high school dreams of getting married fulfilled, her hopes of a family shining, her thoughts of a career dim if not invisible. She looked, but was unable to find a job.

Navy life during the depression was an adventure for the Iowa couple. Her husband and his shipmates, who spent many hours at their apartment, confiscated chickens, butter, or anything else they could get. They often slept four in a bed, not as sexual partners, but as people who understood that necessity is the mother of invention. The Days were based at San Pedro, but spent time in dry dock at Bremerton on Puget Sound, where they lived in a lighthouse. For the first time Jackie experienced homesickness, but she did not rush home choosing to remain close to her husband. Then in 1940 the fleet was sent to Pearl Harbor, and Jackie was pregnant.

She traveled back to Des Moines to have her child. Not long after, Skip suffered an eye injury and was classified 4F. He worked in an ordinance plant on the West Coast the next two and one half years. In December 1941 Pearl Harbor was bombed and Roosevelt declared war. That same year a massive government and industry media campaign persuaded women to take jobs for the war effort. Women responded, two million as industrial "Rosie the Riveters" and 400,000 joined the military. Joining the throng of patriotic women, Jackie worked at the Air Force storage depot and volunteered as a Red Cross nurse's aide. As World War II raged, her husband requested to be sent back to Pearl Harbor, and although his request was denied because of his eye injury, he was reclassified as Limited Service. He was sent to Eulithe, an airplane-refueling base in the South Pacific. While there, he heard of the birth of his daughter Judy. His daughter was four-and-one-half when Harold left the Navy and returned home.

Like the island where he spent several years, Harold Day was described as solid and quiet—a family man. He was a master carpenter and cabinetmaker who came from a long line of men who knew how to make beautiful things with their hands. Claude Day, his father, was a tall, barrel-chested Irishman who loved to play cribbage, read westerns, and detective novels, and ruled his home with an iron hand. His mother, Margaret Murphy Day, was a pretty, shy woman who allowed her husband to be the king of their household and who died too young. Harold had a sister, Jesse Bernice (my mother), and a brother Earl. Earl was the darling of his father. He and his young wife died in a tragic car accident. Their infant son died months later. Jesse Bernice Day, my mother, married Jack Roland Daniels, a meter reader, and through the years gave birth to ten children. Eight survived. Jack, a man with an artistic bent and an eye for women, died at the age of thirty-four leaving my mother with the eight surviving children. I am in the middle—that is, if you can be in the middle of eight.

Harold did not reach out often to his sister or his family—his reach remained close to his own chest and encompassed mostly his wife, his children, and his grandchildren.

After Harold returned home, Jackie became pregnant again and gave birth to twin boys. Tony weighed seven pounds nine ounces and Timmy weighed seven pounds eight ounces.

The morning after their birth, a nurse came in to her room and said, "So, you're the mother of the big twins born breech?"

She answered in the affirmative.

"My," the nurse said, "that must have been hard on the doctor."

Startled, Jackie spoke the first words that came to her mouth. "So, what do you think I was doing? Brushing my teeth?"

Insulted, the nurse raised her chin and left the room. Jackie never forgot the comment, nor did she feel sorry for it. But she often laughed about it.

Jackie returned home with her five-day-old twins, and found her life was much more complicated. Having a quiet daughter was one thing; adding two little boys was another altogether. She soon discovered that being a caregiver for children was a full-time job. The twins were precocious and prone to accidents. As they grew and learned to crawl, and then walk, her form of relaxation and escape was talking on the phone, and this was the twins' cue to get in trouble.

One night she had put them to bed. They had separate cribs and in those days, there were only glass bottles. They jiggled their cribs, moving them close together, crashed the bottles together and then, of course, had beds full of broken glass. Their feet and hands were bleeding before she got to them.

Another time she was talking on the phone. Harold came to the window and told her to hang up as one of the twins was in the neighbor's yard. She assured him there was no way, as they were in bed. He repeated his words and she again denied them. The third time, he shouted that the boys had gone next door and were pulling cat hair out of the neighbor's cat. At nine months of age, they had unlocked the screen, dropped to the ground and crawled over to the neighbors in their gowns that had a drawstring at the bottom.

All the young parents could do was shake their heads in amazement.

Jackie recounted one incident that she would never forget. Harold, who was now a carpenter, kept his tools, including his power saw, in the basement. The twins could crawl downstairs, so they put a gate over the stairs. The first day the twins unlocked the gate, so Harold put a padlock on it.

The next day Jackie was on the phone. Their sister Judy was making brownies.

"Yes, Bernice," she said, "they keep me busy."

She cocked her head. Her eyes rounded. She dropped the receiver and ran. Harold was not at home. She rushed to the head of the steps. The hinges of the gate had been removed and lay on the floor. She rushed down the stairs. The saw blade whirled. A twin stood on either side of the table each daring the other to put a hand under the blade. The boys smiled at her and inched them closer. She said nothing, just kept walking. Tony laughed. Timmy giggled. Their hands inched forward. One more step and she leaned forward and switched off the saw.

Another time, the boys emptied an ashtray full of cigarette butts into a three-pound can of lard and shoved them down into the shortening.

One Good Friday, one of the two-year-old boys went fishing and mid-morning the phone rang and the caller asked if she had a son and when Jackie confirmed it, he said: "Well, we just fished him out of the Des Moines river." Fearing the worst, she was thrilled to discover the boy was merely soaked to the skin.

She later learned he had been jumping up and down on a wooden dock when a plank gave way and he fell with it and had a long trip down the river before he was rescued. Apparently, she never knew the true story—we'll learn that later when Timmy tells his version of this story.

Timmy has a way of telling the truth.

When the building industry became one of prefabrication, Harold Day went into swimming pool construction. His skills as a handyman came to be known and as each season at Riverview Amusement Park neared he was asked to help rebuild the roller coaster, the Ferris wheel, and the boats. After several years of doing this, he was asked to work full time at Riverview and spent the next fifteen years as a valuable employee.

Jackie and Harold could be described as two entirely different types of people—yin/yang, if you will. Jackie—the outgoing, forthcoming organizer, the den mother, one who never missed one of her son's ball games, if she could help it, the tough disciplinarian. When Jackie saw something that needed to be done, she rolled up her sleeves and started to work. Her basic nature was that of an activist from the very beginning. Harold was a homebody, a quiet caretaker, a man who spent his time remodeling and improving the place where he loved to be most—the home on Rohrer Street. They rarely discussed the other's career. They enjoyed bowling, fishing, creating things like a three-floor dollhouse, and raising their three offspring. Their marriage was solid, their love firm.

When Jackie attended social functions with governors, senators, legislators, and presidents, Harold did not join her. Socializing in such a crowd held no interest for this carpenter.

Ironically, the fiercely independent Jackie Day never learned to drive a car. Instead, Harold would drive her to the social gatherings and wait, sometimes not so patiently for her to exit in her beautiful gowns, large earrings, and striking necklaces. This Cinderella figure loved a prince not of the court, but a simple, honest peasant man who understood his wife's world enough to stay away. Her world was not his. Nor did he want it.

Harold provided an important relief mechanism for his wife. He made Jackie laugh when she began taking things too seriously. One incident demonstrates this well. Jackie was working as an administrative secretary for Governor Ray. His personal secretary, Jan Van Note, was a particularly long-legged beautiful young woman. Her looks commanded the attention of most men. The governor, said Jackie, had a "smart-ass male assistant who was jealous because the legislators would come to Jackie and not him to ask to see the governor.

One day when Jackie was particularly busy, she was chewing gum as she worked. She was "busier than a God-damned one-legged man in a butt-kicking contest."

Among other things, she was answering the governor and his wife's mail, scheduling the mansion, and dealing with the Vietnam correspondence that streamed into the office.

This smart-ass assistant came out and said: "I don't think it looks very nice for a woman in your position in the governor's office to be chewing gum."

"I'm sorry, Bill," she mumbled. Then she took the gum out of her mouth and tossed it in the wastebasket and thought: Hell, I'm busier than anyone else in this damn office, and I get called on the carpet for chewing gum! What a crock!

When Jackie went out of the Capitol building that night and walked to where Harold was waiting for her, he knew she was mad and asked what was wrong.

"Oh, hell," she said, "I got chewed out like some kindergartner for chewing gum today."

Just about that time, Jan (the beautiful secretary) came down the Capitol steps and strolled across the parking lot to her car.

She had on a red mini-skirt that showed off her shapely legs. A spring breeze whipped her blonde shoulder-length hair.

Harold watched Jan all the way to her car and then asked, "Who's that?"

"Oh, that's the other secretary."

Harold turned and looked Jackie in the eye. "I'll tell you something, kid," he said solemnly. "You could chew tobacco in that office and as long as that woman works there too, nobody would pay attention."

Jackie laughed for several blocks on the drive home, her anger long forgotten, but not the incident.

Years later, when Jan Van Note retired, Jackie told that story at her retirement party. The audience, Van Note, and Jackie enjoyed the humor of the husband who many did not know existed.

Laughter filled the room, Jackie-style.

Jackie Day could never be only a "stay-at-home mom." Harold's salary as a carpenter was dictated by need and the seasons, and during the winter months he was often laid off. Their income had to be supplemented. She also had a drive to give to the world around her that could not be denied. That passion to give is shown over and over again by her constant voluntary contributions to the world away from Rohrer Street.

Through the years their love remained firm. She believed her husband was amazingly tolerant of her lifestyle. She said that many people didn't know she was married. She never came with a man as an escort unless he was married and with his wife; nor she claimed, did she ever feel the need to have a male escort.

This seems especially striking when she lived in an era when women were raised to be wives, to be partnered with men.

How could a married woman attend social function after social function proudly alone, without a man at her side? Wouldn't she feel incomplete? Weren't women thought of as secondary to the man in their life back then? Wasn't Eve expected to only be a helpmate?

Apparently, not in Jackie Day's estimation. She attended and dedicated herself to her career, proudly, with her head high, gaining respect with each long stride.

But she went alone to these functions with the knowledge that Harold, a man she knew and said often could do anything around the house, was waiting for her behind the wheel of the car ready to drive them back to the modest home Harold and his father, Claude, had built. Yes, while he was waiting, he would have had a few beers, but he was waiting. They would drive back to the house they would live in for fifty years on Rohrer Street in East Des Moines, back to their three children, the mother who lived with them, and their dog.

Jackie, after taking off her gown and imitation fur wrap, would walk into her children's room to tousle their sleeping heads. Later, she would use cold cream to remove her heavy makeup and remove her dangling earrings and necklace, looking more like a queen of natural beauty with each layer of removal.

Jan Van Note & Jackie

Jackie at work

4

Omens

Certain things catch your eye,
but pursue only those
that capture your heart.

~ Native American Saying

April of 1945, when Jackie was twenty-six, she earned her certificate of completion for the prescribed course as a nurse's aide for the Nurse's Aide Corps by the American National Red Cross. Today her uniform hangs in a display case at Camp Dodge.

In 1948 Jackie Day made the news again when she became one of twenty-two area chairmen to organize over fifteen hundred women to make house calls for contributions to the Community Chest Fund Campaign.

By 1950 30 percent of all women in America were in the paid labor force, composed of more than half of all single women and more than a quarter of married women. Jackie was one of the Iowa women counted in that number.

The fifties was the era when Gregory Pincus developed the oral contraceptive, lowering the "whoops" factor for unwanted pregnancies to 1 percent. Activists Margaret Sanger and Katherine McCormick raised money to help the cause. Jackie Day sent a small portion of her meager salary for the research and sat down with Harold to design their newest project—the transformation of their house into a Christmas religious wonder for the public eye.

On December 25th, 1951, Harold and Jackie Day received a telegram from Western Union congratulating them for winning first place in the zone for turning the home that Harold and his father (my grandfather) Claude Day built into a manger. A picture of the home at 1414 Rohrer Street, in East Des Moines shows the Day family. Harold, Jackie, and their three children are bundled up for winter and are flanked by the three kings on their camels. The bright star extends on a pole directly over Jackie's head.

Two years later in 1953 they received another telegram from the chairman of the Junior Chamber of Commerce informing them they won third place for turning their home into a church. Jackie was obviously a proud Christian who loved to show Iowans proof of her beliefs through her loving husband's carpentry and design skills.

Having had few signs of Christmas as a child, Jackie Day was determined to celebrate the holiday with religious respect and the joy of giving. Jackie's grandchildren always remember their grandparents' generosity and Jackie's love for the holiday.

The following year Jackie, in a volunteer capacity, was the educational chairman for the Community Chest Drive helping to raise over $63,000.

Women, at this time earned an average of sixty-three cents for every dollar earned by men. Intelligent women like Jackie knew this fact, fought for more equitable salaries through their voice in women's organizations, but with amazing energy, forged ahead with their sense of community responsibility and volunteered their time for the common good.

Nineteen fifty-six was a busy year for Jackie as an employee of Iowa. In August she flew with Republican State Chairman Don Pierson to the San Francisco Republican convention. Pierson was also chairman of the Republican National Committee's subcommittee on badges. Jackie was the Assistant Chair of Badges.

It turns out that Jackie was one of the busiest people there. She had Pinkerton detectives assigned to her twenty-four hours a day. According to the *Des Moines Register*, she had charge of over six thousand badges. Engravers cut twenty-eight thousand letters.

Seven of the badges were solid gold. Six of them went to President Eisenhower, former President Herbert Hoover, Vice-President Nixon, House Speaker Joseph W. Martin, Leonard Hall, and the president's grandson, Dwight David Eisenhower.

While at the convention, Jackie got into a wrangle with Marcelino Romany, the Puerto Rican who brought down the house four years earlier when he asked a roll call of his three-man delegation in the GOP balloting. Romany attempted to get extra tickets to enter the convention floor. Jackie refused. Romany protested.

True to her nature, Jackie Day won the battle.

One month later, Jackie received a letter from the Republican Campaign Headquarters—Don C. Pierson: "You are the Polk County girl we can always count on to help us out. My sincere thanks for the fine job."

I asked Jackie if it bothered her to be referred to as a girl in that note and she smiled. "That wasn't something we thought of much back then," she said. "But the next time I saw him, I did make sure I called him a boy."

That same year in Des Moines over 400 delegates met at the Hotel Kirkwood to listen to the keynote speaker, United States Representative Paul Cunningham of Des Moines.

A picture of the event shows the crowded room with Cunningham at the podium and Jackie sitting beside him serving a role as an employee of the state.

In May, the League of Women Voters held their annual convention at Hotel Savory to discuss their bylaws.

Volunteer Jackie Day joined Mrs. Donald Lambie and Mrs. C. Dewitt Norton at the head table to lead the discussions.

In January 1957 George Mills, a well-known journalist who would later became an Iowa historian and helped Jackie get money to go to Vietnam, quoted her in an article he wrote about Iowa women in politics. He listed some interesting facts: In 1956 thirteen women were candidates for the legislature—eleven were Democrats and only two were Republicans. All were defeated. No women held positions in either the senate or the legislature. Jackie was a payroll clerk at the time at the Capitol. She was quoted as saying, "Women haven't grown up emotionally—they won't support one of their own sex when it comes to politics. They don't realize their power." Another woman pointed out that women have only had the right to vote thirty-six years while Mrs. Mary Huncke, member of the State Social Welfare board, said, "This is a man's world. I have had men in politics tell me to go home and wash my dishes. Sometimes you hear a woman say that another woman ought to be home taking care of her kids, instead of working in politics. Women keep women from getting anywhere in politics. They just don't seem to understand political organization."

As a woman wanting to keep her hand on the pulse of local politics, Jackie became active as a volunteer in the Good Government Association. She was elected with eight other members to the Executive Committee for a three-year term in the late 1950s. She attended judicial conventions and worked as an administrative secretary in the Iowa House of Representatives for twenty years. She also worked as the office manager for both county and state Republican headquarters.

In an official capacity, Jackie attended five national conventions in California, Chicago, and Miami Beach, and became chief of Volunteer Services for the VA.

At the Republican National Convention in Chicago in 1960 she served as the secretary of the Iowa Headquarters. Women now earned only sixty cents for every dollar earned by men, a decline since 1955. Women of color earned only forty-two cents.

Aware of this decline of concern for women and people of color, Jackie worked closely with Charles Wittenmeyer of Davenport, a delegate-at-large, on the allocation of eighty spectator tickets to attend the convention to Iowans making sure that no color or gender discrimination was involved in the distribution.

In the sixties while Buffy Sainte-Marie, international Native American pop-star activist, and Joan Baez performed their protest songs across America, Europe, Canada, Australia, and Asia, Jackie Day found her own way to further her cause.

In October of 1967 Jackie decided she wanted to join an Iowa delegation going to Vietnam. In the previous two years, the Johnson administration troop build-up dispatched 1.5 million soldiers to Vietnam to fight a war that many found baffling, tedious, exciting, deadly, and totally unforgettable.

Her son, Timothy Day, 19, was one of those Americans. He was a Marine corporal stationed in Da Nang.

One day Congressman Fred Schwengel, an old friend from the Iowa legislature, came into State Headquarters where she was working and told her he was going to Vietnam.

By then her son had been wounded twice.

That morning, the woman she rode to work with who, like her, had a son the same age as her twins, had angered her with the same attitude displayed by most people not directly involved with the war—they didn't want to hear the raw truth about the realities of the war.

She had that on her mind.

Tim had written home saying he had just got off patrol (these were six-man recon missions) and it was a pretty hard patrol. All the members had been wounded, and his best friend had been killed.

She read the letter to her friend, and then turned to her and spoke. "This really brings the war close to home when those you know are getting wounded and dying."

The friend frowned and said, "I think that's terrible. If my son was over there, I wouldn't want him to write me that kind of stuff."

This woman, and many more like her, wanted to deny the horrors of the war. They wanted to play the ostrich game.

Jackie was angered and vowed to make people uncomfortable with truths as long as Americans had troops there. She asked Congressman Schwengel if she could join him on the fact-finding trip to Vietnam. He asked if she was serious about going to Vietnam and she said she was. He indicated it might be possible at a cost of approximately $2,000—the cost for each participating member. She knew she did not have the money. With her usual quick wit, she said: "I don't know one person with $2,000, but I bet I know two thousand people with a dollar."

That day the publicity man in their office put one dollar on her desk, saying, "Jackie, here's your first dollar to go to Vietnam." He also said if she would allow him to call a reporter friend, it would help generate money.

She agreed to let George Mills write a story if he did not use her husband's name, her home address, or make her son look like a wimp who needed his mother.

Tim had already been on fifty-nine range patrols and was wounded twice.

Mills wrote an article in the *Des Moines Register* throwing out Jackie's challenge to raise the money. At the time, she was office manager for the Republican State Central Committee after working for 20 years in the House of Representatives. Prior to this she served as Governor

Erbe's administrative secretary. The official purpose of the trip was to inspect the situation in Vietnam and perhaps to suggest change. Jackie's personal agenda was to gather first-hand information and upon her return to tell her fellow Iowans straightforward, no-holds-barred harsh truths as she saw them.

"If a mother," Jackie said, "should ask the questions in Vietnam, we may get some unexpected and different answers about what our boys see going on and what we at home can do. I believe it is worth a try. Having a mother of one of the boys on hand to listen to what our servicemen have to say when they are lonely or scared, wet and discouraged, could demonstrate that they are not forgotten."

The purpose of the newspaper article was to help get money so this mother could make the trip. It worked. The $2,000 poured in.

Parents of children in Vietnam or in the military, the two leagues she bowled in, and men and women sitting in bars, all sent money. After a while the post office tracked her down and forwarded the mail. She kept track of everyone who sent money and invited them to a meeting when she returned.

When she went, she took ninety-six packs of Polaroid film and took pictures asking the troops to send them to wives, mothers, sweethearts, or others to show they were still alive.

When Jackie left the Des Moines airport, her daughter, Judy and her son Tony were there to see her off. On November 16th the delegation left from San Francisco. All members paid their own way.

Jackie was nervous and excited at the same time. She hoped her son Timmy did not have to fight too many personal battles with his fellow Marines having his mother come to the battlefield. She knew how young men were. Later, in Tim's interview we will learn that he did and that he definitely did not want his mother to come.

When the delegation arrived at MACV (Military Assistance Command Vietnam), they were asked what they were doing there. The Congressmen (Schwengel of Iowa and Cowger of Kentucky) wanted to visit the constituent assembly, the two ministers in the group wanted to see the Buddhist temples and the Catholic shrines, the farmer wanted to see the rice paddies, the industrialist, the industry. Jackie was the only one wanting to visit the troops and have Thanksgiving with the Marines.

According to Jackie her son wrote that he didn't want her to come—it was too dangerous. Later he told her that he still didn't want her to come, but his platoon did because if she could get them out of the bush for Thanksgiving it might be worth it.

Jackie and Tim in DaNang

1967

With French AP photographer

After they landed MACV authorities told her she couldn't go up to the "I" Corp because that's where the action was. She replied, "I didn't come twelve thousand miles to be told no. I'll go if I have to get a Vietnamese on a bicycle to take me."

The military gave in and flew her in by helicopter, and she had Thanksgiving with her son and other Marines.

When the helicopter landed in Da Nang, she was wearing a bright blue floral coat, beads, and earrings. Tim was at the airport and shook his head in disbelief when he saw his mother.

"Gee, Mom," he said. "I would have died if you were wearing combat boots and fatigues."

Jackie chuckled. "Hell, Timmy, I wanted to look like I came from home."

Timmy roared.

On one trip to visit troops they landed in a place covered with red clay. At the time Jackie had long hair and the helicopter blew up the clay, which then settled on her head. They were invited to Independence Palace for the evening; the protocol officer asked if she would like to get her hair done. She answered: "Hell, I don't even know where to eat, let alone where to get my hair done." He told her that perhaps she could go to the hospital where the nurses got their hair fixed.

A Vietnamese woman and her two daughters operated the shop at the hospital. The owner asked if she would mind having her daughters shampoo her hair. Jackie, very much a woman who cared about her looks, of course, had no problem with that. Their fingernails, she said, were three inches long and she had the best head massage of her life. After the shampooing the mother asked how she wanted her hair done. Jackie showed her passport photo and said like that. The woman told her that she had worked at L'Oreal in Paris for twelve years and, ignoring the photo, gave her a beautiful French coiffure instead. It was an odd place to be feeling like a queen, yet she did. She felt like a queen from the east side of Des Moines, Iowa, who had come across the seas with a group of men to investigate a war and she was rightfully proud.

At the reception that evening she was visiting with an officer who was interested in the fact she had been up north that day and asked how she thought it compared with Saigon. She asked him how it was that the Viet Cong could infiltrate the villages so much more effectively than the Americans could, as apparently, the Americans had taken some villages as many as fifteen times. He said the best way he could explain it was like this: When an old lady asked for an embroidery needle, the Viet Cong gave it to her, but the Americans tried to get her to take a sewing machine—an item they would have no idea how to use. In other words, we were killing them with good intentions, but lack of cultural understanding. This was something Jackie heard over and over. As they talked, a huge rat ran between her feet and one of the men in her group asked if she had seen it. "See it! Hell, it was the size of a small dog."

"I couldn't believe you saw it," he said, "you didn't jump or scream."

She hooted. "I was afraid if I jumped the damn thing would bite me and I saw bubonic plague on my trip north that day. Hell, I don't want to take that home as a present."

Jackie thought of this trip as a defining moment in her life. She was fifty-seven. She was a grandmother. When she returned, she began to give talks about Vietnam. She returned with a passion to honor the Vietnam vets who she said lived a hell like none other in the history of warfare for soldiers. It was not a popular stand at the time, but Jackie Day had never been slowed down by the thought of unpopularity.

True to form Jackie spoke what she thought and acted with integrity and honesty.

Always.

Her speaking engagements grew until they reached into the hundreds.

She had come back from the battlefield relentless and impassioned to tell Iowans the truth as she saw it.

On December 25, 1967, one month after his mother returned, Cpl. Timothy Day, 19, was struck in the head and chest by enemy rifle fire near Thua Thien in the north part of South Vietnam on his fiftieth and last patrol before discharge. His mother had been home less than a month. He was sent to a battalion hospital in Da Nang, then to Camp Pendleton in California and awarded the Purple Heart. To this day, he sports a beard to cover the facial damage left by that attack.

When she returned to the States, she was determined to talk in her hard-nosed, assertive manner about a topic many held romantic views about. She spoke to service groups, veteran's organizations, church groups, and anyone else who would listen to her about the harsh realities of war. She was a woman on a mission—a woman whose interest had expanded from the world of politics to the world of war and all of its horrors and ramifications.

She wanted Iowans to face the facts and she spent hours of her spare time driving her point home, almost always without pay and in a manner that did not temper the language that was so natural coming from her. The words "hell," "damn," "bastards," and "Goddamn" were never censored from her daily speech or her public "talks" (as she liked to call them). Her way of talking was as much a part of her as her way of dressing and she never imagined that she would change who she was to project a more polished public image. She never became a politician. She never ran for public office.

Maybe in some way her choice not to do so (many thought if she had run, she could have won) was based on a belief that she must always honor her true self—a proud self that was firmly grounded in her East Side background of poverty and the world of Louis Armstrong who taught her that language as a child.

As years passed she continued to speak at schools, cemeteries, taverns, the Veterans Memorial Auditorium, Masonic Temples, lodges, conventions, dinners, clubs, outdoor meetings, and to the Women in the Military. Her goal was to keep the plight of the soldier in Vietnam in the minds of Iowans. She did not want their stories sugar-coated. She wanted people to understand what the soldiers were enduring so the Iowans would be more empathetic to them when they returned. Her son Timothy, who almost lost his life in Vietnam, recalls later in his interview how he was spit on for being a baby killer. "I was fighting for our freedom," he said, "but the public didn't see it that way."

Jackie Day understood that Americans could not possibly understand the conditions under which the soldiers were fighting. She saw how many Americans were against the war, how they were taking it out on the returning soldier. In the only way she knew, she attempted to spread the word to the public about the soldier's conditions to help Iowans understand.

Typical for Jackie, she took an unpopular stand during a tough time in American history. For some, she succeeded, for others she did not. History has shown how so many of the American public treated the Vietnam vets when they returned home.

Jackie had many other opportunities to hone her skills as a speaker: As an office manager for the Republican State Central Committee and the Polk County GOP Central Committee; the secretary to Iowa Delegation Republican National Conventions of 1960, 1964, and 1968; accompanying Governor Robert Ray in 1976 to the National Convention in Kansas City, and in managing the Good Government Association campaigns for Ray Mills, Ruby Holton, Florence Myers, Reinhold Carlson, Charles Iles, and others. Each opportunity allowed her to use her unedited voice and express her opinion—two things that were very important to her.

In l968 Federally Employed Women was founded to end gender-based discrimination in civil service jobs. Women's movement newsletters and newspapers began to be published across the country. During this same time, people in governmental positions began to hear and pay closer attention to Jackie's speaking and organizational abilities.

In 1969 Donald Johnson from Iowa was the director of Veterans Affairs in Washington, D.C. Jackie met him there on one of her trips to report to President Nixon. He asked if she would be interested in working for the Veterans Hospital in Des Moines in an executive position. Thinking she would be working primarily with Vietnam veterans, she agreed. She took and passed the mid-level college civil service test and was hired to replace the current chief of Voluntary Services. The current chief who had thirty-two years of service had gotten himself into trouble by urging his volunteers to write Congress complaining about the current African American hospital director.

Before being hired for this position, she was the governor's confidential secretary and when it was announced at his press conference that she was leaving to become chief of Voluntary Services at the VA, the current chief hit the roof. Not only, as far as he was concerned, was she not qualified, but she was a woman. How could a woman hold such a position? Especially one who had only been a secretary? His scorn and resentment were blatant.

On her first day of work she had no desk, no phone, and she felt extremely unwelcomed. The environment was hostile and volatile. She was a woman in a man's world—no longer with the title of secretary—she was a threat. The room she was given as an office was packed with old file cabinets, papers, and debris. When her husband picked her up after work, she told him she had made the biggest mistake of her life. He told her to stick it out. She had no intention of quitting but was not happy with the environment she had been thrust into. The chief ignored her.

The other workers didn't know how to treat her. Future boss? Or someone who would soon disappear? She was ignored. She was bored. She was treated as a second-class citizen, yet she had been hired to be trained by him to take his position, something he refused to do.

Unpleasant as it was, she endured for eighteen months, at times cleaning the floor to make the quarters more worker-friendly.

One day as she was scrubbing her office floor, Donald Johnson, the man who had hired her and the director of VA Services from D.C. came in. He was aghast. He scolded her saying there were housekeeping personnel hired to clean up. Without mincing words, she informed him about her situation, about how she was being frozen out, and told him that the office she had been given was badly in need of drapes, carpet, paint, and a good cleaning.

The director listened to her, looked around and ordered everything she asked for, and the office was spruced up. He then spoke to the acting chief. Shortly after that, she was invited to attend staff meetings and further effort was made to freeze out the senior chief and replace him with Jackie.

Her work life, however, continued to be unbearable, so after eighteen months, she spoke again to the director, telling him that this was too big a leap in a career choice.

To ensure that Jackie didn't resign, Johnson made her the assistant hospital director, a job that she felt more qualified for, and one that allowed her a more comfortable position from which to step forward into the chief position.

During her unbearable on the job training period she read manuals, learned about the duties of a chief, read a variety of the women's newsletters that she subscribed to, and bided her time, although she felt her hands were tied.

One day the acting chief came over to her tiny office and asked if she would go to lunch with him. He told her he had decided to retire and asked if she would plan his retirement party. She did so and soon became the chief of Voluntary Services. He went off to fish or golf. She continued to be a woman of action who got things done. That is evidenced by Governor Robert Ray's obvious faith in her abilities. When a war memorial was needed for Vietnam vets, Ray thought of Jackie Day.

Ray appointed her to chair a committee to erect a monument to Vietnam veterans on the State House grounds. The members of the committee were Vietnam veterans, a representative from the V2U and the AMVETS. The current commander of the American Legion was a Vietnam veteran. The committee had regular planning sessions and set a deadline for the following Veterans Day. They also conducted a design contest that was opened to the schools. The designs were displayed at the Iowa State Fair, giving visitors the opportunity to vote on them. The two winners were Jackie's granddaughter Mary Jane Long and Tim Salisbury, an architect from Chicago.

The dedication was held on Veterans Day as planned in conjunction with a Vietnam veteran's reunion. Vietnam vets conducted the program. It was emotional and well attended. Helicopter blades whirled overhead. A jet shot through the sky. Everyone considered it a long overdue tribute—especially Jackie Day.

The money for the monument was raised from private funds and the Iowa National Guard, the governor's office, General Serived, the American Legion, and the citizens of Iowa. There are 860 names of Iowans Killed in Action and Missing in Action engraved on the black granite wall. It is one of the most frequently visited memorials on the Capitol grounds. After all expenses were paid, $35,000 was left over which was turned over to the Iowa Historical Foundation for the acquisition and display of veterans' memorabilia. At Jackie's urging, the American Legion subsequently added an additional $15,000 for this purpose.

Jackie Day, an Iowan woman, proved once again how a woman could get a job done.

In 1969 in Bowe versus Colgate-Palmolive, the Supreme Court ruled that women meeting the physical requirements could work in many jobs that had previously been for men only.

That same year Jackie arranged the initial conference of representatives from women's organizations in Iowa that resulted in Governor Robert D. Ray's establishing the Commission on the Status of Women (ICSW) and she continued to work vigorously to secure its state department status. The Commission was established in 1972 by the Iowa Legislature and is a division of the Department of Human Rights.

The ICSW is a state agency that seeks to assure equality for Iowa women. The ICSW advocates for Iowa women, working to equalize women's opportunities and to promote full participation by women in the economic, political, and social life of the state. The ICSW represents the interests of women in a number of areas including pensions, elder care, sexual harassment, welfare, insurance, divorce, nontraditional jobs, displaced homemakers, pay equity, housing, domestic violence, sexual assault, education, and credit.

Jackie was also instrumental in organizing the Iowa Women's Hall of Fame awards established in 1975 by the ICSW. Each year candidates are nominated by Iowa citizens to honor their contribution to Iowa. A five-member selection committee chooses the final four inductees. Through her fine efforts, Jackie Day earned the right to join a list of Iowa-born women leaders who made a mark in Iowa history.

Besides Jacqueline H. Day, the list includes women such as Arabella Mansfield—the first woman attorney in the U.S., Amelia Jenks Bloomer and Carrie Chapman Catt—two leaders of the Women's Suffrage Movement in the 1880s, Ola Babcock Miller—founder of the Iowa Highway

Patrol, Mary E. Francis—the first woman elected to statewide office in Iowa, Carolyn Pendray—the first woman to serve in the Iowa House of Representatives, Phebe Sudlow—the first woman appointed as a superintendent of a city school district in the United States, JoAnn Zimmerman—the first woman elected lieutenant governor of Iowa, Linda K. Neuman—the first woman appointed to serve on the Iowa Supreme Court, Willie Stevenson Glanton—the first African-American woman to serve in the State Legislature, Mildred Wirt Benson—the first writer of the Nancy Drew Series, and Gertrude Durden Rush—the only woman to help found the National Bar Association, and countless others.

In 1970, the same year that Betty Friedan organized the first Women's Equality Day to mark the 50th anniversary of women's right to vote and the same year that the North American Indian Women's Association was founded, Jackie Day, a descendant of the Oglala Tribe, along with all the members of the original task force from Iowa, joined a second Congressional fact-finding team for President Nixon and returned to Vietnam.

This time she did not have to find money to make the trip. The government picked up the tab.

Nixon wanted Jackie Day to return with the delegation.

He knew that he had the right person for the job.

In August of 1970 Jackie Day and Representative Fred Schwengel (Rep., Ia), Representative William Cowger (Rep.,Ky), the Rev. Heinz Grabia of Davenport, Vernon Shepard, chairman of the Muscatine Country Board of Supervisors, Robert Henry, former mayor of Springfield, Ohio; Dr. Ernest Griffith of Washington, retired dean of the School of International Services, American University, and Allan Schimmel, Schwengel's administrative assistant in Washington, D.C., met with President Nixon.

From 1968-1973 President Nixon had a program of troop pull outs, stepped up bombing, and huge arms shipments to

Saigon.

The 1970 60-page report of data and impressions of the task force declared an "improved situation" in South Vietnam, compared with what the same team found in 1967, but said the Thieu-Ky government still had "serious" problems.

The report called for more U.S. attention to economic and social development programs in South Vietnam, a reorganization of American advisory operations there, and more vigorous pacification efforts. Jackie Day's voice and ideas were firm, to the point, and listened to.

The team proposed that the U.S. withdraw all ground combat troops from Vietnam by mid-1971, and have all military personnel out by the end of 1972. Jackie felt the team had given Nixon some information he did not have before about the potential and need for development of agriculture in South Vietnam, and the need for volunteer services to the people.

American involvement in Vietnam finally wound to a dismal end on January 1, 1973, a week after Nison's second inauguration.

When Jackie returned, her person mission remained—to get the word to the people. This she did with her funny attention getters: "Hey, listen up all you old goats out there." Her jabs at herself: "I'm a clown in disguise," she would say. Then her tone would change to one of a serious information giver as she gave pointed, realistic accounts of what she saw in Vietnam. One can only imagine that her stories match the tone and stark realism that her son Tim relates in his interview later in this book.

Time passed. Jackie worked at her day position and at night to press her firm handprint in the patriotic souls of Iowans. She began to hear through the grapevine that Dr. Jack Wakefield had a dream for a World War II monument to be erected in Iowa. Again Jackie's expertise at fund raising and getting things done was sought after. She was appointed to the committee. They frequently met at Camp Dodge. Since the idea had been Wakefield's, he was selected as chairman of the committee. Unfortunately, he died before the project was completed; however, the dream did not die at his burial. Jackie Day, a champion of the veterans' cause, again served like a soldier with a mission. Using her valuable skills, she helped raise a grandiose $4 million, resulting in the Freedom Flame Memorial. The dedication was held on Veterans Day before an enthusiastic applauding crowd in bitterly cold weather. Jackie wore the same blue coat she had worn to Vietnam. Her hair was stylish and her neck was draped in a Native American necklace of colorful beads. As always, she stood out as a reigning queen at an event to honor men and women who fought for their country.

During this same period Jackie worked as a national Equal Opportunity Investigator for the VA.

In 1978, Jackie, voluntary service officer and public information officer at the Veterans Administration Hospital in Des Moines, was named to the Iowa Hall of Fame. Three other women were also given the award: Dorothy Houghton, who died in 1972, was the first woman president of the Electoral College Board and was known for her activities as national president of the General Federation of Women's Clubs. Carolyn Campbell Pendray of Mount Pleasant was Iowa's first female state legislator. She died in 1958. Ruth Suckow of Hawarden was a writer who frequently portrayed strong women in her works. She died in 1960. Jackie was named to the Hall of Fame for her work on the State Commission for Women from 1972–1976. It wasn't long after this, that a person, whose name is now commonly known, called Jackie Day for a favor—Dan Rather.

At some date in the late seventies a documentary was made and Dan Rather was the commentator. Rather contacted Jackie and asked if she would contribute the AP photos that had been taken of her in Vietnam. She agreed,

53

with the stipulation that the pictures would be returned. When the documentary was made and aired, Jackie received a call from a friend saying they had seen the documentary. She thanked her friend for her comments and wondered where her photos were. To this point she had heard nothing from Rather. Time passed; still she heard nothing. Then one day, she decided enough time had lapsed. She picked up her phone and dialed the number Rather had left with her.

"Dan, she said. "Where are my damn photos?"

The response was upsetting. Apparently the photos had disappeared. Rather apologized, but had not bothered to contact her to explain the situation. She was livid. She understood that things could be lost, but she could not understand that someone would not own up to the loss. Why had she had to call him? She feared she had misjudged Rather.

After this disheartening episode, she never loaned her photos or papers again (until now), nor did she ever bother to view the documentary. Dan Rather had proven himself to be less than she had expected. He forgot or ignored his promise. In a typical Jackie Day move, she wrote him off her list. To Jackie Day, people who struck a bargain needed to live up to that bargain. Nothing was black and white, but there was something called integrity and honesty. She had those qualities and expected the same in others. This ability to judge others' motives was recognized by her old boss and friend Governor Ray. When he needed someone to join a board to help make decisions about whether a person in the penal system was ready to rejoin society, one of the first people who came to his mind was Jackie Day.

She was appointed by Governor Ray to serve on the Iowa Parole Board for six years. The Iowa Parole Board consists of five members, including a chairperson. Board members are appointed by the governor for staggered terms of four years and are subject to confirmation by the senate. The board is responsible directly to the governor and is attached to the Department of Corrections for the purpose of receiving routine administrative and support services.

Iowa law states that the membership must be of good character and judicious background, must include one representative of a minority group, may include a person ordained or designated a regular leader of a religious community who is knowledgeable in correctional procedures and issues, and must meet at least two of the following three requirements: 1. Contains one member who is a disinterested layperson. 2. Contains one member who is a person holding at least a master's degree in social work or counseling and guidance and who is knowledgeable in correctional procedures and issues. 3. Contains one member who is an attorney licensed to practice law in this state and who is knowledgeable in correctional procedures and issues

Jackie, a woman whose formal education ended with high school, served her terms on this board with honesty, integrity, and her usual finesse. She served as chair four of the six years she was on the board. According to all accounts, her street wisdom and intelligent problem-solving abilities made her a humane, savvy interviewer to decide if prisoners should be paroled and/or put into the work release program.

Mary and Louis Armstrong would have been proud of Jack.

5

The Circle

The Circle has healing power. In the Circle we are all equal. When in the circle, no one is in front of you, no one is behind you, no one is above you, no one is below you. The Sacred Circle is designed to create unity.

~ Dave Chief, Oglala Lakota,
Grandson of Red Dog/Crazy Horse's Band,
1930-2005

On a May morning in St. Charles, a small town in Iowa, Jackie Day and I sat in front of our family on a redwood yard swing beside my mother, Harold Day's sister, Jesse Bernice.

The sky was a soft, powder-puff blue with no clouds. A chickadee and hummingbird flitted about the Russian Olive tree.

Cecil, my second stepfather sat in a lawn chair.

Several of my brothers and sisters faced Jackie.

She smiled and began.

"Did I tell you about the old man walking outside the nursing home who saw a frog and the frog said, 'You know I'm really a beautiful princess and if you'll kiss me, I'll give you a night of wild passionate love.

Well, the old man bent down, picked up the frog and put it in his pocket.'

The frog asked, 'Hey, aren't you going to kiss me?' The man smiled as he strolled down the road, 'No, at my age, I'd rather have a talking frog.'"

Everyone roared. Jackie chuckled and patted my mother's knee. Then she looked at my brother Larry who had received an award for bravery years before for saving a woman whose car had slipped into a water-filled ditch.

"I was there, you know, when you were given that award," she said.

Larry nodded.

"The woman never even thanked him," my mother said.

"Yeah, it's just like politics," Jackie said, "They don't give a damn what you did for them yesterday. They only want to know what you're doing for them today."

Again everyone laughed.

"You know," Jackie said. "I was reading in the paper about tips for public speakers. One was to visualize that your audience is naked. Well, here I was last week as the MC at a country club, speaking in front of a group of 80 to 90 year olds and I thought about that tip—now, really, can you imagine all them naked? Dear, oh, dear.

"It reminds me of the story of the daughter who came to the door naked when her mother rang the bell. 'Why are you answering the door like that?' asked the mother incredulously.

"The daughter said, 'This is my love suit. My husband really likes it when I come to the door naked.' So the mother thinks it over and decides she'll give it a try. That night when her husband comes home, she opens the door naked.

"'My God, what are you doing?' gasped the husband.

"'This is my love suit,' answered the wife proudly.

"'Don't look now, honey, but it sure needs to be ironed,' he said and ran."

Larry smiled at our sister Julie. Laughter spilled across the brick patio.

Jackie was in her element.

"So, Aunt Jackie, did you ever have many situations where being a woman was a problem?" asked Julie, tapping a stick on the ground.

"Yeah, well, if I had allowed myself to roll over and play dead, but I've always been so aggressive that I could always hold my own. I think I've told you that when I speak to women's groups that I tell them that a woman in business or government has to be twice as smart as a man, but fortunately it's easy."

Laughter rang out again from the women; wry smiles curled the lips of the men.

"Of course," Jackie continued, "the big differential I noticed was that all the jobs I had throughout my career, if it was filled by a man after I left, the man usually got a secretary and a $2,000 raise. That was one of the discriminatory facts of being a woman in those years. And I was often replaced by men who were paid more while some of the duties were lessened."

"That's a crock," Julie said. She had been a woman with Jackie's same basic nature all her life. I envied her.

"You bet, but that's what it was like then," Jackie said.

"Were your sisters gutsy like you, Jackie?" Julie asked.

"Well, two of my older sisters, Edna and Elna, got me interested in politics, but another one was a homebody with three children. Then she joined the Catholic Church and had three more. It was heartbreaking, in those days, for my mother when she joined the Catholic Church, but then my brother married a Catholic girl as well."

A bird flew to a tree limb. The limb bent.

"My family was very diverse in religion and politics. I had one sister, Elna, who was postmistress for the city of West Des Moines. Another sister, Opal, didn't go to work until she was seventy or more. She worked in a grocery store. I'll never forget her telling the story about the day she went into the lobby holding an umbrella and saw a man standing there with his pants down. My sister went over to him and whacked him over the head and said, 'You filthy son of a bitch, cover yourself up.' The last time she saw the bastard, he was scurrying over the back stone wall."

Jackie paused to let the laughter die down, and then she ended with, "It was better than group therapy. Hell, I bet he never did that again."

The sounds of joy were rich and throaty. Was the story true? I doubt it, but it got her point across—women needed to take control of situations, and she and her sisters knew that fact and acted. Stories, Jackie, knew, touch the soul of an audience, and touching souls was an important part of this woman's code of living. Unfortunately, being assertive is not a quality that all women possess and no one knew that better than Jackie Day who lived with a meek mother with an alcoholic husband.

"Now, don't get me wrong," Jackie clarified. "I really liked working outside of the home. I liked the type of jobs I had. There was never a dull moment. The extracurricular activities that went along with the jobs were exciting and fun. I met a lot of interesting people. I worked at the legislature for twenty years and met people from all over the state. I liked that.

The legislature met biannually, so in between sessions, I usually had another job, either at a Republican state or county headquarters. I had something to keep me busy all the time. I hired the clerks at the legislature, registered the lobbyists, typed bills and amendments.

You know when they made that movie about a town whose people quit smoking, *Cold Turkey*, it was right here in Greenfield, Iowa."

Everyone nodded accept me. Personally, I had never heard of the movie.

"Everett Edward Horton played the role of the old tobacco company chairman. He came to the State House and told us he was fascinated with antiques. When he came into the governor's office and found out the settees dated back to

1885, he was thrilled. One day I took him to the Historic Building. I told him we have the best Indian artifacts collection and fossils around—he loved that. They ended up using the board table from the governor's office in the movie. Later, I received a package in the mail from him. Reporters were gathered around my desk as usual, watching. When I opened it, it was a gift from Horton. They asked about it, of course, trying to make something of it. I had to tell them, that all I did was take him to the historical building. They rolled their eyes like it was a story or something."

Everyone guffawed. Jackie winked. "I never said that Harold would have shot the guy if there had been any funny business."

Laughter again.

"Well, anyway, when the table was returned it was refinished and the Seal of Iowa was placed in the center. It was quite beautiful."

She turned to my mother. "I thought I'd let you know, Bernice, that at East High they're selling brick pavers to commemorate an outdoor classroom that was built called Memory Spiral. I'm going to buy one that says: Those were the Days. I'll have Harold, Judy, and Tony's name put on it. Since they've all been cremated, I don't have headstones for anybody, and I figured that was a way for something to be forever for them. Of course, they've got benches too, but a bench cost $1500 and that's not in my budget. Since we all went to East High, I thought it would be nice."

Bernice, my mother, nodded, patted her shoulder and smiled.

"And you know I'm a past president of the Alumni Association there too. Ron Pearson, the CEO of Hy-Vee, graduated with Judy. Since Hy-Vee gives thousands of dollars to the Variety Club and I've been on the Variety Club for twenty-five years as an ambassador (if you raised over $25,000 and been involved ten years, you're an ambassador). Since I nominated Ron Pearson to the East High Hall of Fame and also to be president of the Alumni Association, I decided to call him and ask for a favor. I told him I would really love to have my name on a Sunshine Coach. Normally, you have to have a single contribution of $5,000. Most of my contributions are small ones. But since this wasn't for me, but for my kids and grandkids, I thought, what the heck, what do I have to lose. He agreed. He's having my name put on a Sunshine Coach. When he called and asked if I wanted Jacqueline or Jackie painted on it, I said, 'Put Jackie and Tim Day and the Veterans of Iowa.' That Sunshine Coach is now rolling around the streets of East Des Moines.

I was impressed. Aunt Jackie wanted her ex-Marine son, a man who stood by her side all through the painful years of her other loved ones' cancer and deaths, proudly displayed before he died, not after. So was the rest of the family.

"That's cool, Aunt Jackie," said Larry, "You know I went to the VA hospital the other day and saw a shelter house there that had the Day name on it. What's that all about?"

Jackie smiled. "You know, I'm always bitching about something," she said. "Well, I bitched for years about the fact they had no shelter house for the patients. There should be a shelter house so patients could meet with their families, have a barbeque, or do whatever they want to do, I said.

"Well, just before I retired I saw carpenters working on the lawn of the VA hospital and I asked them what they were doing. 'You're not supposed to know,' they said. 'None of your business.' Well, they were working on the shelter house behind the hospital. And when I retired it was named the Day Plaza and there's a plaque there that reads 'No Greater Love.' Harold was still living then. He and Judy came to the dedication. That was one of the few times they joined me at a function.

You know when I retired and the Veterans Administration had my retirement party at the Hyperion

Club, I wouldn't let my family come, because I knew if my colleagues were going to roast me and say something bad about me, there would be a fight. My family would never stand for anything being said bad about me."

We all laughed and nodded knowingly as the sun went down and my sister-in-law called, "Anyone for Mother's Day cake?"

Bernice and her parents, my grandparents

My mother, Bernice, and my father, Jack, with my two oldest brothers, Jack Jr. and Larry

My grandfather, Harold's dad, and my mother

Forgive me while I honor my mother, Jackie's sister-in-law.

Jesse Bernice gave birth to ten children. One died in childbirth, another died as an infant. Her husband passed when she was thirty-three, leaving her with no job, few skills, and eight children.

She wrote poetry, was a gardener, a master at working with thread and yarn, the best homemade noodle maker and baker I've ever known, a cherished wife by her third husband, and a loved grandmother and great grandmother. She was a woman who took a different path than Jackie Day, but one, who like Jackie, is to be admired for how she led her life with integrity and loved her children and fellow mankind.

The lyrics on the next page were written after our mother's death by my older brother Larry in homage to her strength and devotion to her children.

The Pictures on the Wall

The pictures on the wall tell it all.
She loved and cherished them all.

She helped them grow in her special way.
Gave them her love each and every day.

Memories have grown, time fades away
The pictures on the wall.

The pictures on the wall tell it all.
Her pride and joy was the wall.

She did her best; we'll do the rest.

She taught them love to carry on.

Then came that day she was called away
From the pictures on the wall.

Now that she's gone, she watches on
Over the pictures on the wall.

Now that she's gone, she watches on
Over the pictures on the wall.

Written for the guitar by Larry Arnold Daniels

Jesse Bernice Day

Julie, Ed, Bea, Larry, jd, Claude, Art, Jack

6

The Guardian

*When we lift our hands we signify our
dependence on the Great Spirit.*

~ Blackfoot, Mountain Crow Leader

On May 11th I drove the winding tree-lined path that led
to the clubhouse of the Des Moines Country Club.

On this particular day, Jackie was giving a talk for the
East High reunion. She had invited me to come hear her and
to meet John Skinner, an old classmate and an award-
winning barber shopper. The chairs surrounding the flower-
adorned tables were filled when I arrived.

When I was married, I'd been a member of this club, so
coming here now felt rather odd, to say the least. My ex-
husband was still a member. Did I miss this part of my
married life? Not at all.

Jackie stood at the podium. She had on a brightly
flowered jacket and black pants, large Native American
earrings, a large necklace—very much the queen. Her
walker stood near her chair. Her white hair was pulled back
into a bun like a crown on her head.

She spoke. Her audience roared, then applauded. I
couldn't help but think of the article Jackie had had me read
from the *Des Moines Sunday Register* written in July of 1975
by Robert Hullihan. Here, let me quote from it again:

"Bejeweled and exotically perfumed like a woman lately come from the throne room of a fanciful kingdom, Mrs. Jacqueline Day sat on the lawn behind the Veterans Hospital.... An enormous necklace of Indian design clattered as she sat forward to eat." Yes, here twenty-six years later, Jackie Day still had that queen-like quality and presence. The fact remained undeniable.

Jackie talked to the crowd extemporaneously with only a few sketchy notes on the podium. Like many comedians, she used herself as a foil to get laughter. She explained that the jacket she was wearing was a hand-me-down gift from a friend, the price tag still on and the crowd roared. She was a natural talker. A well-seasoned speaker, she told a joke at just the right moment, keeping the crowd in the palm of her hand as she delivered her message of pride in being an East High graduate. Her sentences were peppered with swear words, and, sure enough, they sounded like they belonged there. If I had used them in such a manner, they would have sounded contrived, with Jackie they fit just right. The event ended with a standing chorus of the East High song. I felt my soul fill with pride and admiration for this elderly woman who stood with a walker and still had the capability to enthrall a crowd.

Afterward, we sat in the comfortable lobby of the clubhouse and talked. East High classmates John Skinner and Larry Cross drove her to the event. Cross sat close to Jackie and spoke, "When we were in high school, I kept begging Jackie to marry me. She laughed at me every time I mentioned it. Then in our senior year when I got my yearbook back from her she had signed it: 'Marry Me!' But I got cold feet."

We laughed.

John Skinner leaned forward. "I've known Jackie since 1930 when we met at Woodrow Wilson Junior High in the seventh grade. I remember to this day when I first met her. Jackie Day is not someone you forget. She was always the

71

brain of the class. Larry, wouldn't you say she was the brain of our class?"

"Yeah, sure. I think she was one of the upper 99 percent of the class."

John cleared his throat. "I always looked forward to seeing how Jackie did on stuff; she was always an inspiration for me, getting good marks and so forth. We were in music programs together. Mrs. Gramis was our teacher. Then in East High we were in several music performances together. Jackie danced and sang. She has Betty Grable legs, you know. We had a lot of fun. Not that I ever dated her. I was too busy working to date in those days. I had to work to help support the family of ten kids. It was the depression, remember? Jackie was very popular, with the guys and gals and the teachers. Everyone respected her brain power and energy. She was always full of desire to better herself. She was known for her enthusiasm, drive, level of participation in events, and her excellent grades. Course she was a looker too—that didn't hurt none. Those legs, you know. I'd say it's always been a privilege to know Jackie Day. She's the kind of person you could trust."

John leaned back on the sofa, thought for a bit, and then spoke softly. "Course, no one would ever guess that Jackie was overcoming an inferiority complex by her actions given to her partly by those older sisters who were always having her wormed when they showed up for a visit. You know, when she was a senior in high school she was diagnosed with TB. Hell, I remember that Jackie never had a study hall because she always took extra classes. She was also a member of the honor society, a cheerleader, in many operettas, and on the newspaper. The principal actually punished her for taking the extra classes by making her pay more than the other students and, of course, she didn't have the extra money, but she came up with it somehow or other.

"When she talks, she always says that getting involved is the secret. Life shouldn't be a spectator sport is what Jackie says, and she's right about that. Yes, Jackie had more adversaries than most, but she sure came out on the top. She was the only child in her family to finish high school. And with her positive attitude and her uncomplaining personality, no one would ever guess what she has overcome. And the interesting thing is that no one I knew would ever try to intimidate Jackie Day. She always had that sense of being in control. I'll never forget how she looked in those hand-me-down flapper dresses with the low bodice cut, a looker; that she was. Yeah, she was the type of young person everyone expected to succeed. Did you know that when she was twelve she knocked on doors handing out political handbills to help her father keep his garbage-man job? Well, that's the kind of person Jackie was and still is. At fifteen she was frying and selling five-cent hamburgers at a booth at the Iowa State Fair. She spent most of her time trying to convince her customers that there was meat in the bun. She always was a character, a convincing character at that."

When the reporter, Robert Hullihan called Jackie "a master mechanic for the Iowa Republican Party, the woman who knew what bolt needed a bit of tightening, what county chairman needed a squirt of soothing oil," he most likely hit the brass nail right on the head. "Jackie is a sparkling woman of uncut realism and the truth comes from her unadorned."

That's the quality that endears Jackie to so many who have met her through the years, and most likely made those who got on her wrong side shudder in her presence. Hullihan wrote: "There are men in high places who once stopped by Jackie's desk for a little down-to-earth advice. There are men fallen from high places who may wish they had."

But Jackie won't admit that.

"I just talk smart-aleck. I never had much influence," she says.

The Robert Hullihan article relates in delightful journalistic prose a tale of how Jackie Day drew a shrewd, faster gun than even more well-known celebrities. The story tells of when she dry-gulched Gene Autry, the old cowboy movie star.

Back in 1964 Jackie arrived in San Francisco at the Mark Hopkins Hotel that was owned by Autry to set up the Iowa headquarters of the Republican Convention. The problem was, wrote Hullihan, Autry was easing his saddle sores in the very suite that Jackie had reserved for the Iowa headquarters.

"The manager said he certainly wasn't going to call the owner of the hotel and tell him to move out," Jackie recalled. "I said, 'If he doesn't move out by morning, he will damn well wish he had.'"

As the 200 Iowa delegates began to arrive, Jackie simply gave them the number of Autry's suite and told them it was the place to pick up their tickets and credentials.

For the next several hours delegates trampled around the halls on Autry's floor beating on his door. Autry finally figured out he was facing a faster gun. He saddled Champion and rode off into the sunset. Jackie Day moved in and set up headquarters on time.

Yes, when Jackie Day had a goal, she went after it with skill, dedication, and a street-wisdom that was hard to outdraw and no matter who you were, you might as well not stand in her way—not when she was positive she was right.

Jackie at eighteen

THE
Interviews

Part II

*I have seen that in any undertaking it is not enough for
a man to depend simply upon himself.*

~ Lone Man, Teton Sioux

The following interviews are transcribed from tapes.
Because they are all direct quotes, I have chosen not to place
what each person says in quotation marks. By doing this, I
hope to eliminate reader confusion. I believe they stand on
their own as brush strokes that add more clarity to the
portrait of Jackie Day. When these interviews were
conducted, Jackie was still alive, so they speak of her in
present tense.

7

Governor Robert Ray

A Woman Who Told You Straight

*All birds, even those of the same species, are not alike,
and it is the same with animals and with human beings.
The reason Wakan Tanka does not make two birds, or
animals, or human beings exactly alike is because each is
placed here by Wakan Tanka to be an independent
individuality and to rely upon itself.*

~ Shooter Teton, Sioux

On March 16·, 2001, snow swirled outside the window of
my now deceased sister Bea's home in the countryside of
Norwalk. It was a blizzard, the second blizzard that
threatened to keep me from having an interview with former
Governor Robert Ray. But this time I was determined not to
cancel the appointment, and thankfully, Ray was willing to
meet me at his office downtown.

After gunning my little Chevy Cavalier's engine to get
up the small hill in front of the house and saying thank you

to the front-wheel drive vehicle, I drove cautiously into the city.

Before I entered his office I watched Ray and his personal secretary choosing original paintings. The exchange was lively, warm and a decision was made. Ray's opinion won out over hers, but I was glad to see that her opinion was asked, mulled over and discussed.

He leaned back in his chair, put fingertip to fingertip and began.

What do you remember about first meeting Jackie?

The first time I recall hearing about Jackie Day was when I became active in the Republican Party. Jackie was involved, I think, then on the state level. She was a person who I had been around politically. I loved to talk to her and get her take on what was happening politically. Jackie was always wonderful as a conversationalist and was a woman who would tell you straight what was happening. That would have been back in 1956 when I ran, so I met her probably in 1955. I have great respect for her. She was never one who just came to work in the morning and typed letters and went home at 5 o'clock. She had an intense interest in her job and how it related to the political party, and politics in general. I think she dearly loved that. When you love something with a passion, you do it extremely well. She was one that people like to go to; they liked to visit with her and she liked to reminisce. We'd kid her of course about the East Side—you know, Lee Township against the world. And she was very much a part of that world. She was proud of where she came from and where she lived and had great pride in the East Side, but there wasn't anyone with whom she couldn't speak and talk to and she was well respected by people in politics and those people who financed politics. She was at ease with all of them.

I don't know anyone who didn't like to see and talk to Jackie Day.

I went on the State Central Committee (SCC) in '58 or '59. I had a rather competitive battle to get elected to the SCC, and then I became the Republican State Chairman. Jackie and I worked very closely together. I don't know exactly what her title was, probably secretary. Today, of course, that would be administrative assistant, but that was back a long time ago. She was one who kept active, not just doing perfunctory things. She was very knowledgeable about politics, one I could go and get straight answers from. She was always cooperative too. I don't think I ever asked her to do something where she said no, or if she couldn't do it, had someone else do it. That's when we got fairly closely acquainted. That's when I was Republican State Chairman.

Then I ran for office for governor and after I got elected I sought her out. She had been secretary to Norm Irving when he was governor those two years. I felt she would have some gubernatorial experience, knew the office and how it was run. I didn't have any staff when I got elected. Jackie gave me advice and she agreed to come in and sit at that front desk where everyone had to get past her before going anywhere else.

It's fun thinking about Jackie. I remember having a concern about whether her and my personal secretary, Jan Van Note, would get along. Jan had worked very hard for me in my campaign. I thought there might be some conflict between Jan and Jackie, but I don't think there ever was—at least, I'm not aware of it, and I think they became friends. So that worked out quite well. Jackie always had a way with her—she made everybody feel comfortable and important. Her background helped her, I believe, enormously because she knew you didn't have to come from the wealthy ranks to succeed. She'd seen enough people come from what she would call the lower East Side and succeed. But she also understood the problems of not having lots of wealth. The worst thing about the East Side, and I still think this exists, is that people have a terrible time believing that they're not looked down upon, or that people think that they're inferior, because they came from the East Side.

Part of that I think stems from people growing up with nothing; then they make it and they move to the West Side. Jackie always had a good understanding of that and she was always very proud of the East Side and has always lived there.

Personally, I love the East Side. So many real—what I call "real people." East Des Moines people are stable, moderate, and good people. I got acquainted with that part of the city when I was in law school. I was able to get a full-time job with the *Des Moines Register*. I was hired as a district manager for carrying the papers.

My first district was up East 9th, downtown past Euclid, then it branched out on both sides, over the river and east about the same distance. I recruited carriers and grew very fond of that area of the city.

How did you view Jackie's role as a woman working in a predominantly male environment?

Jackie never had to take the back seat to anybody, nor did she. She always left the impression she was comfortable in a man's world. She could talk a guy's language no matter where that guy came from.

When I started the Commission on the Status of Women, Jackie was very active in its formation.

In fact, one time Iowa got an award during that period for being one of the top states in making advancement for women.

I didn't broadcast it because I didn't think we'd done nearly enough.

But we tried, we worked at it and Jackie was a significant part of this activity.

The Commission is very important. The designations that have come from that are very important in recognizing leaders, Jackie being one of them.

I was the one who first appointed Jackie to be on the parole board and I am very proud of that.

Here was a woman who grew up with little, and she knew what created some of the problems for people who wanted to achieve and wanted to pull themselves up by the bootstraps.

She understood those that didn't have to do that as well—the contrast—she had great perspective on life and what it takes to succeed and fail.

I thought she was an outstanding member of the board because she knew how to ask the right questions, she knew how to look at and determine what the best criteria were to judge a person's ability to succeed, and I think she really enjoyed the role too.

Her contribution was very valuable.

Did it ever occur to you that Jackie might be uncomfortable working on the committee?

No, never. Jackie Day could enlighten or educate people with a higher education or sophistication. I have no doubt about that. How many of the members were lawyers? I don't know. I suppose quite a few. But that would never have bothered Jackie. She was her own self. She thought through things, made decisions, had opinions, and was not shy about expressing them. But she also knew the delicacy of "where to" and "where not to" express them. That comes from having years of experience in politics.

There were people who want to hear things and she could tell them. Then there were others she shouldn't tell for a lot of reasons—because they'd misunderstand, they'd misquote, or go out and sell that opinion wrongly.

She had good judgment in that respect.

Do you ever wonder if Jackie should have run for political office?

When I first met Jackie, women weren't running for office. I would love to have had her run for office. She would have been great. Take, for example, if she had run for legislature and been elected, which she might have been in recent years—I think she worked over there. She would understand that arena and the governor's office workings too. She has no problems forming an opinion. She could stand toe-to-toe with those people who get loud or boisterous or demanding or express themselves as if they know all the answers. I can just hear Jackie cutting them off at the knees. She'd have been great.

What about Jackie's way of expressing herself? Would that have been a problem?

I don't know what it is that makes you accept people for what they are and some people can speak in a tongue like hers and somehow you think that's just right. For any other person, it would sound vulgar. I think it's the personality, the persona that goes with it, and that's part of what you love about Jackie. She says it the way she believes it and she says it the way you understand it and I don't think people are offended by her method of expressing herself.

What would you say are Jackie's strongest attributes?

That's easy. You can always trust her. Strong personality. Liked politics. Was influential. Loved her family. She had some terrible tragedies and it takes a strong person to have the kind of attitude she's had to overcome those tragic circumstances. She loved those kids. She was faithful to her husband. She has a lot of good qualities, more than I can even think of now. She and her husband seemed very compatible. Different personalities and different occupations, but —I didn't know Harold that well—they seemed very compatible. Their roles were almost in reverse—Jackie attended functions alone at night; Harold was never there.

What would you say makes Jackie Day tick?

She loves life and believes she can leave a contribution to her community, to women, to politics, and to her family. She has good, sound values and good goals. I think she wants to be, could be, and I believe, thought you should be—active, a contributor. I always like seeing Jackie. Always like visiting with her. She is always colorful in her expression. You can discuss things with her. I don't think she ever got mad if you disagreed with her.

I don't remember ever disagreeing with her, but it's one of those things where people have input into decisions; you can't go every way to favor everybody. She was always supportive of me and my decisions, whether she agreed or disagreed with them.

Also, Jackie was a person who was fun to work with. I don't like to work with people where they're not on the same level. We worked as equals and I hope Jackie would think that—I believe she would.

I always thought everyone in my office was extremely important.

Were you surprised to hear Jackie was having a biography written about her?

Yes, it surprised me pleasantly, because I didn't know anything was happening. I think hers is a rich story. Rags to riches might apply. I'm not talking about money. I'm talking about what's really rich in life—things like friendship and being a good person.

How much money would you want to trade a friendship? I don't think there is enough, is there?

With Billie Ray, Governor Ray's wife

Gov. Ray on left, Jackie, Mary Brubaker & Unknown

8

Dolph Pulliam

Dressed Like a Butterfly

*We learned to be patient observers like the owl.
We learned cleverness from the crow, and courage
from the jay, who will attack an owl ten times its size to
drive it off its territory. But above all of them ranked the
chickadee because of its indomitable spirit.*

~ Tom Brown Jr, *The Tracker*

On a cold winter day in December I drove to the Drake University Field House to meet Dolph Pulliam, the athletic director. Drake is my alma mater and I enjoyed driving around the beautiful campus before parking on the street across from the field house. Pulliam has an infectious joyous spirit, one that is rare and refreshing. After a warm handshake, I was directed to sit in a chair across from his desk.

After telling him a few brief things about myself, and admiring his office, our interview began.

Tell me about when you first met Jackie Day.

I met Jackie—it was September or October of 1969. I had just graduated from Drake and started work at the local television station, TV 8. My assignment was as a news reporter and my first beat was the state Capitol. I worked with a fellow by the name of Charley Lacon. He was going to take me around and show me the State House. He took me there and went off to do what he does. I was left to saunter around and sauntered into the governor's outer office. When I walked in, lo and behold there's this lady sitting behind the desk and she's dressed like a butterfly. She has some of the most colorful clothing on and her makeup and her hairstyle, and, well, she just bubbled. Her face was lit up with adventure and a smile. It was one of the most welcoming things I ever saw. When she saw me walk in at six-foot four-inches and two hundred and twenty pounds and black, she just got up and welcomed me as if she had known me all her life. I didn't know who this lady was, but boy was I affected by her. She sat me down and we talked. She said, "Tell me about yourself."

"Well, I played Drake basketball," I said.

"Yes, I know all about you going into the NC final four."

We went on and on.

Then she asked, "What are you doing here today?"

"Well, this is my first day with TV 8 and I'm over here working the state Capitol now with Charley Lacon."

"So, are you going to be coming regularly to the State House?" she asked.

"Yeah."

"Well, son," she said, "You need someone to show you around and I'm just the one to do that. Come with me."

And she took me throughout the State House. She took me into the secretary of state's office. She took me into the Supreme Court. She took me through every office there: The treasurer's office. The comptroller's office, and she

87

introduced me to all these people. Then she took me down into the governor's world down below her office and introduced me to all the people there, and she said, "Now, I'd introduce you to the governor, but he's not here right now. When he gets back, I'll introduce you to him. Anything you need, you just come to me and I'll help you out. If you need to interview somebody, just contact me and we'll set up that interview for you."

And I thought: You've got to be kidding! I was twenty-two years old, had just graduated from college. And that's how my relationship with Jackie began.

Every day when I went to the State House that was my first stop, always. I came out of the State House with some of the greatest stories. As a matter of fact, one day we were talking and she glanced behind my back, grimaced, and said, "Oh!"

The attorney general had been in, his name was Turner, I can't remember his first name, and he had just marched out of the governor's office with a huff. I saw him and said, "What's with this guy?"

"He's mad about something," she answered.

So, I thought maybe I should go over and see what he was mad about. I went over and talked to him. Turner said he was mad about something the governor had done, and he had decided he was going to sue the governor. I asked him if he were willing to say that on camera, and he said he was. And I thought, Oh, my God! What a break! So I get the camera set up and we sat down and did an interview with the attorney general and he confirmed that he was going to sue the governor and I had my first exclusive. In my time working with Jackie I had many exclusives.

Another time when the legislature was in session, Jackie Day had set up a surprise for me with the speaker of the House. Jackie sent me up to the House and I walked in and sat with the reporters. I'm sitting next to Charley Lacon and the speaker saw me come in and he hit the gavel and said to all his state representatives, "We have a celebrity here." I thought, Oh my God!

"And we want to introduce him." After he did, everyone stood up and gave me a standing ovation. That was quite a thrill. Jackie Day set that up.

Through the years we became very, very good friends, as you can imagine. And I had many opportunities, because of Jackie, to access Governor Ray. Then, later, Governor Ray and I became friends and are still today. Jackie started all this.

It was such a deal at the State House that the other reporters started to complain of my having collusion and that it was unfair how I was being treated so well up there and they weren't. Even my own television station TV 8 thought I got an unfair advantage. "You're able to get news stories that no one else is able to get. Even our own reporters can't get those kinds of stories," they complained. "You're able to get that kind of stuff because of your friendships you've created up there," they said. So they pulled me off. Yep. They took me away from the State House. Everyone thought, even the governor, they should have seen it as an advantage, but they didn't. Everyone knew I was able to keep a secret unless they told me that I could use it as a news story and many people came to trust me and confide in me. But they pulled me off that beat.

What's reporting all about? Well, I had taken reporting to a different level. They said, you've gone beyond reporting. You've used your celebrity status to help you get into these people's offices and that's not fair. Well, that was a bunch of bull. A bunch of bull. A couple of years later Governor Ray left office and Jackie took another job. I think it was with the Veterans Hospital with the Veterans Administration.

Shortly after she got there she called me and said, "Dolph, I got something for you to do over here."

"Oh, what?"

"Just come over and let's talk."

So I went over.

"Now I'm going to tell you something and if you'll be embarrassed by this and you don't want to do it, now I'll understand, because no one's ever done this before and I don't want to put you in any position that's going to be embarrassing. But if you think you can do it, then I'd like you to."

My curiosity was piqued.

"Jackie, what is this that you want me to do?"

"We want to start a tradition and have a Christmas party for the veterans at the hospital."

"Well, Jackie, of course I'll help," I said innocently and quite enthusiastically, I might add.

"I want you to be Santa Claus," she told me, looking me directly in the eyes.

My eyes rounded. "You what? You want me to be Santa Claus! Santa Claus!"

"All you would have to do is go to all the rooms of the sick veterans who can't come out to the celebration. You go into their rooms, some are going to be very sick, some may even be dying, but I want you to go in there and see them."

"Jackie, what are you talking about? I'm black! There's no black Santa Clauses!" I said incredulously.

"You would make a great Santa Claus," she said.

"Oh, Jackie, this is not going to work. People aren't going to go for this. I'll go to the rooms and these people will be expecting to see a white Santa and they're going to see me!"

"Dolph, Calm down. Calm down. What you will be doing is making their day. We could send a white Santa Claus in, and, yes, that would be nice and he would give them a present and that would be nice, then he'd be gone. But if you walked in there and you gave them a present and you talk with them, they're going to remember that for the rest of their lives and they will say, "That was a black Santa Claus!"

"I kept thinking, oh my God, oh my God."

"Jackie," I said, "I think you've gone off the deep end."

She laughed. "Oh, Dolph, we've got to do it, we've got to."

All I could think was, Oh, dear me. I thought about it and I thought about it, even to the day that I was supposed to do this I was still ready to back out. So, I thought, okay do it, and sighed.

I was picked up and we went to the hospital. When I went in Jackie gave me my Santa Claus suit and I thought: Oh boy, this is going to be something. Staff members took me down to the hospital rooms. All the way they reminded me that I would see some very sick veterans, some not so sick, and some would be terminally ill. Some aren't going to feel like talking or anything—they won't even know that you're there, but we'll take you into those rooms anyway. I thought: Oh my God, what am I doing? What am I doing? But, okay, I'm doing it.

We get to the first room. There's a black guy in bed and he's an old guy, looked like he was about ninety-years-old. I stand outside and ring the bell and say in a loud voice, "Ho! Ho! Ho! Merry Christmas! Santa's here!" I inhaled a deep breath of air and burst into the room.

The man in the bed yells, "Oh my God, he's a black Santa Claus!" He starts to laugh and continues to laugh and I can tell that I made this guy's day. You know, at his age and mine, it just opened us both up and we went from room to room to room. Some veterans had tubes in their arms and most of their life was gone and they would look at me and "Oh my God," they would laugh or a smile would come across their faces and some even cried and some wanted to sing *Jingle Bells* with me as I sang. I went on to other rooms and when it was over I want to tell you I felt I was Santa Claus.

I realized that I had brightened their worlds, made them smile or laugh, and gave them and myself something that was new and different. Jackie Day started that tradition. It had to be in the early seventies, the first year after she left the State House. Through the years her grandchildren helped pass out presents. That was a lot of fun and an experience I will always remember.

Jackie Day had that uncanny ability to put you in a situation that if she thought you could succeed in it, even when you didn't, she could convince you that it would be fine, it would be fine. And, in this case, I did it, and it was more than fine. That tradition continued every year while she was working for the Veterans Administration; it was an event all the staff and I looked forward to.

Jackie has always kept in touch. She never forgets me at Christmas time. I always receive a card. I remembered years ago she called me to give a speech for the Lee Township Club that meets once a month (I think they all graduated together from East High). I went to the Bishops Cafeteria at the Southridge Mall and spoke to the group and we had a great time.

I've heard Jackie speak several times throughout the years, at the Kiwanis Club and various other places, and she is a stand-up comedian. Jackie can tell stories that can blow you away. They are funny because her life has been so funny with so many escapades and what have you. You know she can tell incidents that happened to her and Jan Van Note in the governor's office and the things they got into and kept the governor out of, or got the governor into. I tell you it was just hilarious to hear some of those things. She is a wonderful speaker and storyteller. Her life is filled with stories that touch your heart and mind. [Unfortunately, Jackie Day did not write down her speeches.]

Jackie Day is in a class all by herself. I have not met anyone like her, where she could meet a stranger and instantly that stranger becomes a friend. And you can warm to that person and you feel like you can open up and confide to that person. She was sort of a grandmother to me instantly. I've not been able to compare her to anyone that I've met and I've been around Iowa now since 1965 and I've not met a lady who has all the characteristics that I feel Jackie Day has. There are some other people who come close to her, but there's nobody who has been that close to power (as close to as much influence—national as well as local) as Jackie Day has, who has continued to be an open, joyous person who can both keep secrets as well as give you little anecdotes that intrigue you. Jackie will be the only one in my lifetime who I'll ever meet like that. It's just a special, special gift that she had and has. She's everybody's friend.

Did you ever meet Harold?

Harold? Yes, I knew Jackie was married, because we talked about him, but I never had a chance to meet him. Of all the many functions we went to, I never met him. I knew he existed, but I never saw him.

Speaking of functions, I remember once we had a private dinner at Governor Ray's mansion (the first governor's mansion). I had chosen a young lady to take with me and she was very nervous, so I gave Jackie a call and told her how nervous Linda was and told her I was sure this wasn't going to work.

"Oh, me and Billie (Billie Ray) and Jan (Jackie's friend and colleague)—we'll get her and keep her calm, don't worry," she assured me.

"But she's trying to back out," I said.

"You just bring her," she said, "everything will be fine."

And when we got there Billie, Jackie, and Jan took her under their wing and they hugged and socialized and we all had a great time. I remember that time well. It meant a great deal to me.

We had some special, special times together.

In your opinion, what makes Jackie tick?

People. If you tell Jackie something can't be done, you've just fired off the first shot and you're at war because Jackie is the kind of person to have none of that. It's a challenge to her. Anything somebody says, we can't do this—we can't get that, well, take the Vietnam Memorial built up there on the state Capitol grounds, for instance— lots of people pooh-poohed that idea. They said it was too expensive and said it couldn't be done. Oh, my word, but that didn't stop her. She got that attitude turned around and got it done. Yes, she did. That's the kind of person Jackie is. She is motivated by the challenges in life. She takes on individuals too—like someone like myself when she first met me—a young person (not immature, but young) without a lot of confidence in a new environment. She would take you on as a project. She would build you up, strengthen you, and all of a sudden you have more confidence in a room full of people. That's what she did for me. That's the kind of person Jackie is. She has a bigger heart than the world and she doesn't have—well, she's like color blind—you know—that was one of the things—because in 1969 it was still—you know, racism was still prevalent and as a black person I was very self-conscious walking into a different environment and wasn't able to be open and "Wow"—no, I wasn't like that. But Jackie was the kind of person that it never occurred to me that she even thought about my color and I was so impressed with that. She could disarm me, cause I was armed thinking that we'll never get beyond color or race, and … phew ... with Jackie there was none of that. She would treat me just like she would treat the governor of the state of Iowa or any other dignitary or celebrity. She was just like that and again, those kinds of people are rare to find.

My basketball coach taught me something very special too my senior year at Drake. Our team was winning and we had just gone to the national tournament and there were a lot of requests for us to go out and talk to different groups and what have you. One day my coach came seeking me out.

"Dolph, I have all these speeches that I'd like you to give."

"Oh, coach," I said, "there's no blacks in those towns and when I drive in those communities the police or someone might beat me up! I may never be heard from again."

"Dolph, you'll be fine. Just fine."

"But coach, I just can't do it. I'm not going to go. I'm not going to go."

"Now, son," said the coach. "I'm going to teach you something that you need to remember. I'll tell you how God gives you the ability to know whether you're safe or whether you're in harm's way. I want you to listen. Wherever you go—and you'll go to these different towns I'm going to send you to—the minute you get out of the car and meet that first person who's there to meet you, you grab that person's hand and you shake it and look that person right in their eyes— that's how God will let you see and know. If their eyes tell you that you're in danger—leave. You just turn right around, get back in your car, and you leave that town. No matter what happens, I will defend you, I will stand up for you. But if their eyes are warm and tell you that you are welcomed and safe, then you go on and talk—go with your instinct, your feelings."

"Okay, coach!" I said, amazed at the simplicity of the advice.

And I went around these little towns all around the state of Iowa to speak following that advice and it worked.

When I met Jackie for the first time, her eyes bowled me over, because they were so alive and there was so much adventure in those eyes and then you got to her glorious smile, and I thought, Oh my goodness!

With Jackie, I had a good feeling from the very beginning.

What was the type of relationship you observed between Jackie and Governor Ray?

Friends. A working environment that was very casual when it was just the governor, Jackie, Jan, White Wooley, and Dave Ullman. It was a causal, laid-back situation with no holds barred. Everything was open and if somebody wanted to play a joke or a trick or say something funny, everybody laughed. It was like everybody could kick back and relax. That's the kind of thing I saw between Jackie and Governor Ray. She would straighten a tie. She would touch him. And many times people don't allow you to get close and when you do get close, they will stiffen up, or what have you, especially if you touch someone.

I watched as Jackie would handle Governor Ray and it was almost like she had permission—it was, well, accepted—and he didn't even notice it many times, because he accepted it. It was like Jackie was there, and Jackie was going to make it right, and so she would straighten a tie, she would brush down a coat. She would find his glasses. She would say things to him that I wouldn't have said, and he'd listen and sometimes I heard him ask, "Are you sure, Jackie?"

And she'd say: "Hell, yes, I'm sure! You do what I tell you to do!"

And I'm thinking: How does she do that? How does she get by saying that to the governor? And one day I asked her about it.

"Hell, I raised that little kid. I'll tell him what I think!"

She was like a wise mother to him, and he would laugh and shake his head, because that was Jackie and he listened to Jackie. I was impressed and thought, Wow! What a neat, neat relationship and working environment to be in.

I take it at work she didn't clean up her language?

Oh, no! No! I had to get used to that. I didn't swear a lot, but she sure did and everyone accepted it, because it was Jackie Day.

Jackie Day came along at a time when I really needed someone who could get me started out on the right foot. Or, I came along at the right time and met someone who could mentor me, motivate me, inspire me, and take away some of the defenses that I had built up about people—even races of people. She was able to knock those defenses down and give me the ability to clearly see a wide spectrum of issues and things. I am eternally grateful to her. She helped to change me when I needed to be changed, and when I was starting to close down and close in, she helped me open up and trust people. That's an amazing gift to be given.

You've heard of the term Renaissance man? Well, Jackie Day was a Renaissance woman as far as I'm concerned. You don't find a lot of people like her. She would have been a great politician, for any office she wanted to run for. She possibly could have been the first female governor of the state of Iowa if she had pursued it.

Why do you think she didn't?

You know, I don't know why she wouldn't have pursued that. Maybe it was thought in that era and time women could never achieve such a thing. I don't know. But knowing Jackie, if someone would have said that, she would have taken the challenge. But I don't think anyone asked, Why don't you run for political office? I don't know why. In fact, that would be one question to ask her. Why didn't you go for it? I sure would have voted for her and campaigned as well. I sure would have.

Did you know about her Native American heritage?

Oh, yes. We talked about it and I shared with her my own Cherokee background. There's a lot about Jackie I don't know, but there's a lot I have seen over the years. I'm honored she told you that you have to talk to Dolph. That's very special.

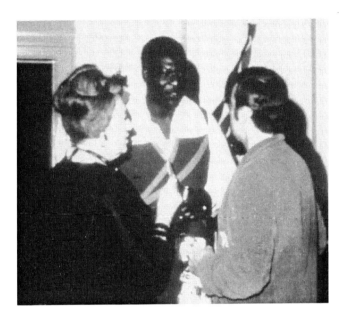

Dolph and Jackie

9

Governor Terry Branstad

A Pioneer

We do not want riches but we do want to train our children right. Riches would do us no good. We could not take them with us to the other world. We do not want riches. We want peace and love.

~ Red Cloud, April 1870

I met with Governor Terry Branstad on a Friday afternoon at his office in West Des Moines. It was a crisp, clear day in the suburbs. As always, I was amazed at how the area had changed since I last lived nearby.

Governor Branstad told me he was pleasantly surprised to discover that a book was being written about Jackie and looked forward to reading it one day. I shook his hand and told him that my brother Larry said to tell his wife hello. His son used to babysit for their children when they lived on the South Side. He assured me he would, crossed his hands in front of him and waited for my first question.

How long have you known Jackie and in what capacity?

100

Jackie's been an active Republican for a long time and I think my recollection (and this is kind of before my time) she worked for Governor Erbe and for Governor Ray. I met her when I first got started in politics, probably back as early as when I was in College Republicans. That would have been late 60s, '68 or '69. Then I went away to the service. Sixty-nine and seventy-one I was in the army. I came back and went to Drake Law School. I didn't know her all that well then. I was just a kid and she was a prominent Republican. But then I got to know her a lot better when I was in the legislature and then as lieutenant governor and then governor. I worked with her. She served on the Parole Board, and then I appointed her to the board of the Law Enforcement Academy. Also, she played a very key role (she's always been close to the veterans) in heading up the effort for the Vietnam Memorial my first year as governor. We kicked that off and dedicated that in '83 or '84. And she did the same thing for the Korean Memorial. She's worked very closely with the Indians at Tama. I went to the Pow Wow a couple of times with her.

When you think about Jackie, what do you think about?

I think of somebody who is a very dedicated, proud American citizen. She loves her country. She loves her family. She is a great patriot in the sense that she has always been dedicated to honoring and respecting those people who were in the armed forces and helped preserve the freedoms and the liberties that we cherish as American citizens. And that's something I believe in. I served in the army during an unpopular time during Vietnam and I guess you appreciate people like Jackie because it was not a fun or popular time in which to serve in the military. That's what I appreciate so much about Jackie, that she was committed to those Vietnam veterans making sure that they received appropriate thanks for their service.

101

What would you say are Jackie's strongest attributes?

Well, first of all, she's very personable and outgoing. I don't think she ever saw anybody that she didn't like. So, that's one of the things—her personality. She's had plenty of hardships and problems in her life, but she always seems to have a very positive attitude and she's fun to be around, and she always treats everybody as her friend and treats everybody with respect and dignity. I appreciate that. I had a great teacher who taught me the three R's of good government: Rights. Respect, and Responsibility. We all want our rights protected, but, also it's important to respect other people's rights, and the idea of the responsibility of being a good citizen and giving back. Jackie has always been one to give very generously of her time, talent, and resources to help the state, to serve in different capacities and to work for causes that she believes in. So, I just think she's a great role model of the kind of citizen that we want to have in this country and somebody who is one of the most fair, decent persons I've ever met.

Think about the picture of women in Iowa—the history of women in politics. What would you say about Jackie's place in this venue?

I'd say she was a pioneer. She was really involved. She's not a women's libber—I would say—but she was ahead of her time. She was a woman who didn't complain. She did a lot of work that she probably didn't get recognition for. She was a real pioneer in showing that women can and do play an important role in our public life, and she did that, was involved in all that, long before I came along, and continues to do that up to today. So, I think in being a pioneer, she has been an inspiration to many younger women to get involved, because they can make a difference. There is an opportunity in the political process for women to play a more and more prominent role. She was involved long before most women gave any real thought to being politically active.

What is your fondest memory of Jackie?

Well, the Vietnam War Memorial situation. I was a brand-new governor. We didn't have any money and we wanted to honor and recognize the Vietnam veterans and Jackie said she would take on this project and work with the veteran organizations and get the money to build the memorial. We didn't put any tax dollars into it. That was a pretty neat thing.

I believe her granddaughter designed it. I was and am very proud of that accomplishment, and we did the very same thing with the Korean Memorial. The state donated the land, but that was it. Remember, I came in at the onset of the farm crisis and money was tight.

The state didn't have any budget. It was incredible how she got the job done, considering the circumstances. Then she graciously did the encore—heading the effort for the Korean Memorial too. Mind you, that was a volunteer, unpaid position and effort.

We were one of the first states to build a memorial and did it about the same time as the one in Washington, D.C. That was quite an accomplishment.

If you had one thing to say about Jackie Day, what would it be?

She's a role model of what a good citizen should be. She's someone who cares about people and treats everybody well. She gives generously of her time and talents to help others and has a positive attitude. I think that captures what Jackie's all about, unselfish, caring. In Iowa we are blessed with a lot of friendly, outgoing, caring people, but I think

103

Jackie Day is extra special because she has always seemed to have a tremendous amount of energy and enthusiasm to get involved to help other people and help especially the overlooked and the downtrodden.

That's another thing, the Indians who have not always been treated very well and the Vietnam veterans. She always had a real heart for helping those people who may not have gotten the respect and recognition they deserved. It's easy to follow the popular, but that wasn't Jackie. She was not one to follow the crowd. She's always been one to do what she felt was the good and right thing to do, and that may not always have been popular, but I certainly have respect and appreciate someone like Jackie who is there for people who have given of themselves for this country or the community.

Many times Jackie would be the only woman working with men, like most of the veterans were men. Sometimes the Vietnam veterans are obviously a lot younger than she is, but she related with them very, very well and they respected her. I think she's a person who has always commanded respect. She was always somebody that I felt like I knew before I knew her, because she'd worked in the governor's office. I aspired to that someday, and she was somebody who was a leader, and somebody I looked up to and respected as a College Republican trying to get started. That was the years when a lot of people wanted to tear down the establishment and I remember saying: "I hope someday to be part of the establishment." I always looked to Jackie as a great role model as a leader in our party and a leader to really respect and look up to.

Do you think Jackie was ever intimidated by being a member of the Parole Board when many of the members were lawyers?

No. There have always been a lot of lawyers on the Parole Board. The chairman at that time was a lawyer from

104

Olewein, Walt Sour. There was an African-American woman from Fort Madison too. I remember Jackie went down to Fort Madison for a retirement party or a recognition party for this woman who served on the Parole Board, and she was maybe the only white person who was there at this event. Was she bothered by a difference in educational background and board members with a higher degree? Well, I honestly don't know her educational background, but I do know that she had wonderful people skills and did a wonderful job. Jackie was never one to be intimidated.

What do you think is Jackie's passion?

A love of people. She loves her country. Loves her family. I mean, she loved life. I guess she is one of those people who have lived life to the fullest in the sense that she has interacted with many people and made a real difference in their lives. She's a very caring person. So, I think, concern for others and making sure they're treated with respect, those are the things that drive her. She's a very compassionate person too.

Serving on the Parole Board is a tough job where you have to make a lot of tough decisions and say no a lot. The job also takes somebody who is compassionate and understanding. She's got that compassion. She's got that combination of compassion and inner strength that it takes.

Many women are being taught today that it's a mistake to be so giving, that it could lead to being taken advantage of. Where does that idea fit in with what you've said about Jackie?

That is true sometimes. Some nice people who are caring and giving are taken advantage of. One of the things I think Jackie has done a good job of is trying to make people who did the work and didn't get the recognition and respect they

105

deserved receive a thank you, recognition, and respect. That has been one of the shortcomings of our society. Jackie's attitude was always that we don't do enough.

One of the things I started as governor and what I'm real proud of, is we started the governor's Volunteer Award Program. Each year we would recognize what I would call the "unsung heroes" and Jackie is truly a leader in Iowa's unsung heroes who gave so much of their time and talent to help other people and never got any recognition for it. There are so many of them in the state.

So what I started was a governor's Volunteer Award Program. Every year I asked departments of state agencies and state government to nominate people who had done things they were aware of to receive that award. I personally handed out those awards. I feel that's one of the best things that we ever did. There are so many people like that and Jackie Day is a leader among those people. Jackie was a statewide leader, but some of the others are only in their local communities or in their churches or on a smaller scale. I think that a little recognition and respect can go a long way.

Do you think Jackie took needed time for her family?

Yes, well, like I said, she is a family person.

She is very committed to her family and cares deeply about her family and like anybody there's nobody who's not had some disappointments or some painful experiences in the family. I think that Jackie understood the importance of having the balance in your life between being publicly involved, but also the issue about being involved with your family.

It's a delicate balance we all kind of struggle with. There are a lot of people like her, like me, who have been very active in politics.

The time you give to help others takes time away from your own family. I know I have tried to be there for my

106

kids, but there are also times when I had a busy schedule and I was gone.

The more you're in a public position or public responsibility, it's tough. I remember what my wife said one time: "You know, I'd like to be treated like a constituent."

10

Roy Park, Ph.D.

Santa's Tale

Out of the Indian approach to life there came a great
freedom, an intense and absorbing respect for life,
enriching faith in a Supreme Power, and the principles of
truth, honest generosity, equity, and brotherhood as a
guide to mundane relationships.

~ Luther Standing Bear, Oglala Sioux, 1868–1937

Roy Park, a former professor from Iowa State, met me at
the Drake Diner on December 11, 2001, for lunch.

My instructions were to look for someone who looked
like Santa Claus or Kenny Rogers. I arrived first; when he
walked in the door I knew I had my man: White full beard.
Robust. Pleasant good looks and demeanor. A
straightforward look in the eyes. Yes, this must be Roy Park,
Ph.D.

He looked just like Santa Claus, maybe not as much as
my older brother does, but close.

Oh, yes, I have my favorites.

We sat, ordered, and began a most jolly and sincere interview process in the noisy café.

So, tell me about your relationship with Jackie.

I became acquainted with Jackie because she couldn't drive. I drove us from her house to Rockwell City or Fort Madison—whatever the case may be—based on our parole interviews.

What I found was that I learned more in talking with Jackie Day going to and from our assignments than I did at many of my course assignments at Iowa State working for my Ph.D. I was a professor at Iowa State in Industrial Engineering. I have a Ph.D. in Human Resource Management.

Let me give you an example: One thing you know about Jackie is that she has a very direct way of saying anything, and I can recall one time traveling back from a really trying time with some "not caring" prison guards and being very frustrated that they weren't doing what they should be doing.

I talked to Jackie about this and her answer was, "It is our responsibility to assure we do our job well. If we do set a good example, others will follow."

That advice made me more comfortable.

She had a way of not blaming others. Instead, she would find a way to turn the situation around so that change would be the result.

What an amazing way of looking at life.

She believed in change and spent much of her life bringing it about.

I also remember her evaluations of many of us on the board. While Jackie wasn't a woman's libber, she certainly understood women's rights.

She would watch carefully our members interviewing women at the women's institution.

One particular man who has gained much acclaim in the United States was so sexist in his comments and questions that it was an embarrassment both for Jackie and me.

We would plot together on how it was best to share our concerns to help this individual become a more effective member and certainly how to be more appropriate with our female inmates.

Something else that's important, Jackie is a Republican. I was chosen for the board because I was a Democrat. What was interesting was that her background from birth to most of her life was very democratic in my opinion, and her philosophies were very democratic. Yet, she was a very staunch Republican.

I share this information because we would discuss politics or things of value as we traveled and I also kind of chided the Republicans. I'm kind of a centrist, but Jackie's views were always about caring about people. It made no difference what their status in life was—their nationality, their sex, their race, their age, or their religion—she cared about people. That attitude was very infectious; it was very difficult not to care in return. Her affection for Indians was just unreal. She knew what particular burial responsibilities and rituals were, what the sweat tent symbolized—I could go on. She was remarkable in her knowledge of Indians and their way of life. She loved them and they in turn truly love her.

For two years, I worked with Jackie on the Parole Board. I had said I would do one year, but stayed on for two years to a large degree because of Jackie. Why?

Jackie Day was such a positive influence. To watch her in an interview with an inmate to determine should the inmate do more time or should the inmate be considered for release was an education. She had a rational, logical, and caring mind, but was still a conservative view as to what should happen as to release or retention. Just to experience that with her was an education.

We had some very talented folks on the board at the same time. One, Jim Greisner, who is being considered for a district judgeship, I had the utmost respect for.

As I look at Jackie's life from my perspective—following her childhood, the war, Bankers Life, and I didn't know her in those roles, only as a Parole Board member. The time I was on the board, there were two females, Jackie and Virginia Harper. The other five were males. The legal mix had to be a certain number of Democrats and a certain number of the prevailing party, in this case, Republican. The mix was four Republicans and three Democrats.

Theoretically the decisions made are independent of male/female positions. But the problem we found was some of the male contingents on the board viewed female inmates different than male inmates. They asked questions that were both sexist and outdated. Jackie's talent was to make sure people understood that the women should be treated just as male inmates were as to whether they got parole, not to whether they had a pretty face or (how did she say it) a "cute butt," but rather, had they served enough time to satisfy the obligation of their sentence, and had they prepared for release to society. Jackie had a very strong talent at that.

There was some concern at the men's prisons that a woman might be viewed differently—as kind of a "weak link" on the board. That view did not hold with either Jackie or Virginia. They were viewed as very strong members. In fact, there were certain crimes that inmates would have preferred to have anyone but Jackie on the panel.

We would break into panels of three. We had seven members, but in those situations a panel of three was selected to interview and we would try to have one female on each panel. We met several times. We were at every institution every month. In addition to that, we would go to the Parole Board office and evaluate files to determine should there be an emergency required for release occasioned by prison overcrowding.

111

There was a court order that said we could only have so many prisoners in our system. So anytime the prison cap was breached by too many inmates, we would have a responsibility to parole a certain amount to get that below the prison cap. Jackie most often took the lead in that. Why? (A) She was willing (B) She had the right talent. And, (C) Walt, who was our chair, couldn't always come from his home in eastern Iowa to Fayette County. She was a very valuable, active member of the board.

What would you say made Jackie tick?

I would often be awed by prison guards assuming authority over inmates. Jackie said it reminded her of the days at the State Fair when she was a child living quite near the fairgrounds. She would see people who had no jobs during the year, but during the State Fair would be parking attendants or ticket takers. They would get a pith helmet and a stick and all of a sudden they were God! All you have to do, Jackie would say, was give someone a pith helmet and a stick and they are transformed into something they ought not to be. I guess too often we have people in this world, be they guards, be they CEOs, be they a cop on the beat who see their position elevated far above what it should be in reality. I guess to answer simply what makes Jackie Day tick, is her tremendous sense of fair play. I think that's remarkable— fair play, no matter what.

Why do you think Jackie didn't run for political office?

I think Jackie's self-image might not have been the same as other people's image of her. I don't think she saw herself as a politician and I'm not sure she would have really enjoyed being a politician. I think she rather enjoyed making politicians do what politicians ought to be doing. She was more of a "behind the scenes" person with very strong views. But sometimes having strong views is not accepted in either party. She was in the best of all worlds for Jackie. She could speak her mind, and that she did very eloquently and sometimes very directly, but she didn't have to couch her words as maybe a true politician must.

Have you ever heard Jackie give a talk?

No. I have never heard her give a long speech, but I have heard her many times in short, informal venues. She has the audience in her hands. I, too, am a public speaker. She could have topped me financially and in every other way, there is no doubt about that. She has a very strong talent in communications.

Jackie Day is not only special, but she makes people she comes into contact with feel special because you're you. If you're doing well, you can't leave her without feeling good. And if you're not doing right, she'll give you a lesson on what you're not doing right in.

Where would you say that Jackie fits in with the history of women?

Jackie was ahead of her time. Long before some should have known better, Jackie was saying: "No, you should call us women, not girls and they are blacks, not boys." I was fortunate to be enlightened by a couple of students as well as Jackie.

Jackie's assertiveness was a blessing and a curse.

It was a blessing for people who were enlightened, especially management people—who understood that that's the quality that makes things happen. But, then there were the people who felt their own self-importance by virtue of education, experience, or such—who felt, How could anybody dare access either my skills, my abilities, or my position?

113

But having said that, if I could remold Jackie in any way—it would be never to take any of the assertiveness or self-confidence.

That's what makes Jackie. And those poor people who didn't understand it, truly shame on them. They don't know what they missed.

What is one thing you would like to see in print about Jackie Day?

Jackie sees all people for what they are as human beings, not what they are by way of position, rank, or authority. She asks that society treat these people fairly, whatever that might bring: The good, the bad, the ugly. She tells it like it is; she lives it like it is, and is willing to stand up for her beliefs, and is willing to support your beliefs as long as you interfere not with others in a negative fashion.

What would you say about her relationship with her husband Harold?

I saw a couple seriously committed for a long number of years, each willing to help the other in whatever way possible. I think Harold was not comfortable in some of the settings of Jackie's career. I think many times he stayed home much to Jackie's concern and dismay because she would much have preferred to have Harold with her. He would often drop her off where she was talking.

I think she would have liked to do some of the things she did that he never saw. They had a loving/caring relationship.

11

Jackie

Cracking the Glass Ceiling

We live, we die, and like the grass and trees, renew ourselves from the soft earth of the grave. Stones crumble and decay, faiths grow old and they are forgotten, but new beliefs are born. The faith of the villages is dust now...but it will grow again...like the trees.

~ Chief Joseph, Nez Perce
1840–1904

Jackie and I sat in her favorite Mexican restaurant sharing a rich piece of flan. I explained that I had a set of questions to ask. I was curious how Jackie would respond to them.

There was no doubt in my mind that she would be honest and forthcoming in her answers.

I sipped my coffee. Jackie told a joke to the waiter. We all laughed and I began.

By the way, one of the greatest pleasures of this process was how much I got to laugh when I was with Jackie. That alone taught me much.

Jackie, what individuals had a significant impact on your life?

The people who've had the most impact are people I met in my political career. One would be Vern Martin, state chair of the Republican Party. He was the type of individual that although he didn't drive, he came in from Newton on the bus every day to be the Republican state chairman in Des Moines. He was a wise person who answered every piece of mail he got, and always did it in a very unique way. For example, if he would get a request for a subscription to *Reader's Digest,* he would acknowledge it and thank them for bothering to write. When he wrote letters to Republicans, he always put a little plastic elephant at the top of the page. If he wrote someone who had good fortune, he'd put a little plastic four-leaf clover at the top of the letter. Yes, he was very unique in his approach to people and life. He would always say: "Give me one rose today, be it pink or white or red. I would rather have one rose today than a hundred when I'm dead." He was just that type of individual, very nice to be around.

I may have told you that at one of the Republican Conventions where the candidates were invited to a luncheon with platform guests (the events usually were held at the Veterans Auditorium) I was in charge of ordering the food and other preparations. At the Vets Auditorium, at that time, you had to use the Des Moines Catering Service. You had no other option; they had a contract and you had to employ them. This particular summer event I had ordered the food: cold cuts, potato salad—that sort of thing. After the meal the platform guests were given the opportunity to speak and the candidate for governor at that particular time was called on. His first remark was, "I don't know who ordered this food, but it was the lousiest meal I've ever had." And, of course, I was terribly embarrassed. Mr. Martin knew I had ordered the food, so to take me off the hook, he replied,

"I'm sorry you didn't enjoy the meal, but if you'll see me afterwards I'll be happy to refund what you paid for it." It was, of course, a free meal. I always loved the old man from that day on because he really took me off the hook. When he wrote me when I worked at the legislature, he would often glue a picture of me on the envelope and write, "To the lady who everybody knows." He had a unique approach and his kind way of treating people had an impact on my life.

Another person would be Fred Schwengel, the Congressman from Davenport who was responsible for me having the opportunity to go to Vietnam twice. Going to Vietnam with Fred Schwengel was probably my fifteen minutes of fame. He was an athletic nut who did six hundred and fifty push-ups every morning. One of the group who went with us to Vietnam said it wore him out to watch Fred do his push-ups every morning. He was the type who would go through the airport carrying someone else's luggage (that's when it was a kindness).

He was a unique person too. He was a real student of Abraham Lincoln. He had an amazing collection of Lincoln memorabilia, even had the suit that Lincoln was wearing at the time of his assassination. In D. C. he would oftentimes go in the basement of the legislature under the statue of Lincoln and recite the Gettysburg address. People would think Lincoln was talking to them. He had an impact on my life.

Then there's Bob Ray, a person I've also always admired. I think I've told you the story of one of the things Bob Ray did when he was governor. I answered the mail, the telephone, and scheduled meetings for him. It was very busy in the early days when he was elected governor. One duty was being asked to throw out the first ball at the Oaks game in the summer. We had gotten an irate letter from Williamsburg from a young boy who said he had saved his money all winter to buy a baseball glove. When he sent the

117

money in, they had raised the price of the glove and he couldn't afford it. When I took the letter into Bob Ray, I said I don't blame that kid for being angry. If I'd saved my money all winter for a baseball glove and couldn't get it, I'd be mad too. Bob said, "Oh, Jackie, you're just an old softy." When he went to throw out that ball at the Oaks game, they gave him an autographed baseball, a glove, and a bat. A day or two later he buzzed me and asked what he had on his schedule for the afternoon. "Nothing important, just the same old crap," I told him. He said he was going to be gone for a couple of hours and left without saying where he was going. The next day I asked where he had gone. Well, he had gone to Williamsburg and given that kid the ball, the bat, and the glove. No publicity. Nobody knew he did it. That was just the kind of sweet person he was. He really cared for people; his wife did too. They are really high-class people who care for others, their friends, and their family.

So, I guess these are some of the most influential people in my life.

Do you believe society restricts women? Do you believe you have the same freedoms, privileges, and protections as men? Why or why not?

I think women have had to come a long way and I think we are coming a long way. But in the early days of my political career men didn't even think you should have the right to vote, let alone have the right to have anything to say about elections and that sort of thing. Women in particular who have been influential are women like Mary Louise Smith who was a dear friend of mine. I worked for her election as National Committee woman. She did a wonderful job. She was the first woman to be the chair of the National Republican Party. I do think women have had to fight to get an equal place in a man's world, because basically it's a man's world. I have factiously repeated the old saying: A woman in politics or business has to be twice as smart as a man, but fortunately it's easy.

So, you think today it's still a man's world?

I do think so in many areas. I do think, however, many women have cracked the glass ceiling. They haven't destroyed it completely, but they have cracked it. In athletics, in politics, in business—women are making their presence known. They have to do twice as good a job in many instances, but they are doing it.

Do you consider yourself a feminist? Why or why not?

I don't consider myself a feminist to this degree: I never wanted a man to give me any concession because I was a woman. I always wanted them to consider me for the job and being able to do the job as well or better than a man. I don't want to be favored because I'm a woman, but I want to prove to them that I'm as good in that particular position as any man. No, I don't consider myself a feminist; I consider myself "female."

What's your definition of a feminist?

To me feminists in many cases don't feel like men can do the job anyhow. Many feminists (not all) feel superior to men. I think that's a fallacy. I don't think we (women) can afford to feel superior to anybody; not only from the gender standpoint, but from the racial standpoint as well. Once we get to feeling so full of ourselves that we think we're superior to anybody or any race or gender, then I think that's a defeatist attitude—rather than a feminist.

What are your current health circumstances Jackie?

Well, I was very healthy until recently. I developed diabetes and had a stroke caused by diabetes. I've been doctoring many years for hypertension. Many of the members of my family have died from cerebral hypertension. I suspect that's what I had when I had the stroke. I had never before been diagnosed with diabetes, but it was a diabetic stroke. Since that time I've broken a hip, broken my arm, and severed several bones. The hip broke first—then I fell and had to have a hip replacement. I think it was a matter of osteoporosis causing the weakness of the bones.

Even as a child I had primary TB. Of course, they always said I had worms. I was always a fainter, puny, skinny.

I have Pernicious anemia and had blood transfusions. But you know as we get older, we can cope with the physical disabilities—it's the mental disabilities I find very difficult to deal with. People suffering from Alzheimer's and memory diseases—that is much more debilitating than broken bones.

When you experienced menopause, what kind of experience did you have? Were you prepared?

I never felt any symptoms. I didn't pay attention to it. It was an inconsequential period in my life. I do know there are people who suffered all kinds of symptoms, but I fortunately, didn't have them.

I never had PMS. I hear women talking about PMS today. To me, that's: Putting up with men's shit. I've done a lot of that in my day.

If you could change your current circumstances, what would you do and why?

Well, it would be pretty difficult to change my circumstance at this late stage of my life. I'm eighty-years-old and I'm content with where I am right now.

I'm still active enough to be on the Law Enforcement Academy and the Iowa Centennial Commission. This is enough activity to at least give me something to look forward to. I'm fortunate enough to have family here that I see frequently so that I am content with who I am right now.

[The Iowa Law Enforcement Academy is an independent agency of the state of Iowa. It was created by an act of the Iowa legislature in 1967 to maximize training opportunities for law enforcement officers, coordinate law enforcement training in Iowa, and to set standards for the law enforcement service. The Centennial Commission is set up to provide scholarships for seniors.]

If you could change your past, what would you change? Why? If so, how?

If I could change my past, probably the only thing I would do, maybe, is to save for a rainy day. I've always just lived day by day and never really considered the future to the extent that I prepared for the future or made investments that would ensure a more comfortable old age. I don't know that I would do anything else differently. I would have to be a hell of a lot smarter to do anything differently.

If you could change the world, what would you do?

Well, I would remove all prejudice. Prejudice exists where you least expect it, and some people who profess to be really Christian are very bigoted and narrow minded, not only when it comes to races, but to gender. It goes back to what I said earlier, if you can change the world—probably the two things I would change are better communication and better understanding.

121

How do you feel about your life and accomplishments and what accomplishments are you most proud of?

I think I've been very fortunate. I've had some wonderful, wonderful opportunities. I've taken advantage of most of them. I think that's the thing most everyone has to do. And that is to take advantage of opportunities when they're offered. I think I probably regret the things I haven't done a lot more than the things I have done. I think you regret things that you haven't done.

Going to Vietnam I think of as my most important achievement. Especially, having the opportunity to go at a time we were putting a man on the moon. Here's a country fifty miles wide and one hundred miles long that the French had been trying to conquer for thirty years and we were over there and suffered some of the heaviest casualties that had been suffered in any war, and yet we couldn't do anything to offset communism in that country. Having had the opportunity to be there during the war I feel I had an insight into what was actually going on. I feel going gave me a better understanding of what our troops went through.

I don't admire our government for our involvement, and I think that our troops were just players sent over there in a real untenable position and asked to do things that former military soldiers were not asked to do. I just feel like it was an exercise in futility and I think the people who were in power at the time knew that. You will find the Congressional Record in my papers. Fred Schwengel reported to Congress about our trips to Vietnam and what we discovered were the flaws and the weaknesses of our involvement over there.

How would you like to be remembered?

Probably as a person of integrity and honesty. My grandma told me years and years ago that you can lock your door against a thief, but you have no defense against a liar. I think honesty is one of the things—and we don't always appreciate or welcome people who are brutally honest. For example, if someone asks, How do you like my hair? We expect the answer, I think it's beautiful. But if you tell them, I've seen your hair look better, it doesn't always make you popular. But to me, honesty is important. I always want to be remembered as being an honest person.

Would you consider yourself a luminary? Someone who is a source of light to help others to develop their capabilities to the best of their abilities?

I have tried to do that in that I've never been jealous. I think jealousy is the green-eyed monster. I caution my grandchildren and family not to be jealous of another person's accomplishments. I don't know if I've ever been a luminary in anyone else's life, but I certainly have never been jealous of a person's accomplishments. I consciously try to avoid being jealous of other's accomplishments.

Do you think you are a person who helps others?

I try to help others, but oftentimes people (if they seek your help that's one thing), but there are many people who resent your help. I've tried to be selective, not to force my opinion or help on someone who doesn't really want it or need it.

When someone asks your age, do you tell them?

Absolutely. I'm proud of my age. I am proud that I have existed eight-two years. I never thought that I would live that long and I still am of the opinion that there must be a

123

reason for me to be around. The easiest way to resent your age is to regret the things you haven't done. I still want to "do." No matter how long your life is, it's never long enough to accomplish all you want to get done.

12

Marine Corporal Timothy Day

The Vet's Story

Let us put our minds together and see what life we can make for our children.

~ Sitting Bull

Sunday, lunchtime. Timmy Day had already played eighteen holes of golf and I had visited with his mother Jackie. We met on the East Side and I was hungry and curious to talk to my cousin who I hardly knew at all. Our greeting was warm, but reserved, and I was glad we were meeting over lunch. Months before Tim had lost his wife of thirty-one years, Linda, to a long bout with cancer, and I could tell from his eyes that he was still in mourning. We chatted, and then I directed the conversation, not to his mother, but to Vietnam. I wanted his take on the subject.

From past experiences with Tim, I recognized that he had inherited his mother's straightforward, no-holds-barred way of speaking. By listening to him, I suspected I could get a better understanding of how his mother, with her tough speech and use of everyday examples to explain a point, presented the issues of the war to Iowans back when the war was still raging. I wasn't wrong. Tim did not disappoint me; there were times when I thought that I heard Jackie whispering to her son over his shoulder: Say it how you feel, son—don't hold back. Celebrate that we are different, not the same. And Timmy Day did just that—or did he?

Tell me about your war injuries, Tim.

Well, I was shot three times, the last time in the head. One bullet went into my eye here and went out the back of my head. I was also shot in the neck, and it blew out my back. That was Christmas Day, 1967. Cease fire. I had about fifteen minutes left and I was coming out. I had ten minutes left before the choppers came. Lance was in a tree scouting out a clearing for us to run through. There were thirteen of us and we got hit with a ninety-man gook regiment. Seven of the men had been in the country less than a week, and one of my men got a little wild and opened his mouth when he should have kept it shut and me and Lance had to pay the price for it.

The gooks heard him and found us. They stood looking up at Lance—he was about ten yards away from me. Four of them kept looking up the tree and Lance had his back to them, so he didn't know they were there. I had the choice of either yelling out to Lance to turn around or open fire on them and turn the fire on me, so I decided to bring the fire on me. It didn't do any good. They killed Lance and they shot me, but I killed four of them. I didn't know there were ninety of them behind these four. It turned out to be a reinforcement company. But the rest of my men got out, and I got out too.

First, I was in a hospital in Da Nang, then I went to Japan for a month, then I was in a naval hospital for about eight months. Next, I went to Camp Pendleton for around five months.

126

I was a guinea pig for the doctors. Since I got shot in the head, I had doctors trying out all sorts of stuff, trying to rebuild your ear—stuff like that. The idea was, If we fail you may die, but hell, you were supposed to be dead anyhow. So they kept operating. They were successful with some of them. Of course, those doctors made some people live who should never have lived to begin with, but they killed some people who ought to have lived, but you kind of live with that I guess.

After I got out of the hospital, I became an instructor of recon at Camp Pendleton, teaching kids how to go over there and get killed. I met my wife, Linda, a month before I got out. They were trying to get me out on a medical discharge. I knew Linda about a week and she called and asked if I wanted to get married and I said, Maybe. She said come back in February, I have everything arranged. So I went over the hill and got married. Two months after that they discharged me from the service (sent me back home and told me not to come back).

When I was an instructor, I had to go back into the hospital a lot. When the bullet went into my head, it shattered my skull and so I had bone splinters come down, that's why my beard's sunk into my head. I have 50 percent disability benefits now, used to have more. It's the same old story. Vietnam vets beat the hell out of WWII veterans as far as benefits go. We were the new kids on the block, so we got more benefits than they did. Now the Gulf War veterans took over from the Vietnam veterans. You know how they always say, "the forgotten veteran"? Well, they think they don't have to help us anymore, because they have the Gulf War veteran to deal with, so we suffer. [Now, of course, there are the Iraq veterans.]

You know, the country don't really care about the people. There's two kinds of people in the United States, there's the realists and then there's the people who think that our government's a God, the government workers can do

127

nothing wrong, they don't say wrong, they don't lie to us. You know, the "If you don't like it then, by God, you leave" attitude. Well, I fought for you people and I think you guys suck. You killed me dead for no reason, then, excuse me, you didn't give a shit whether I died or not. But some people think that's blasphemy, I mean, they tickle me.

Just like when I was overseas and came back, that's when it hit me. Free love. I had a woman spit on me. I was a baby killer. It's amazing how you preach freedom, but I sit here looking like I do now and you want to fight *me* because of freedom. Yeah, people will fight you in the name of freedom.

When I went overseas I didn't know what free love was. Jesus Christ, are women selling it now? I mean, Jesus Christ, they were giving it away in high school!

We laughed. I could tell that Timmy was enjoying how his way of putting things had my full attention.

Did you make any friends of hippies when you came back?

Oh yeah, I know plenty who didn't and wouldn't go to Nam. I tolerate anybody as long as they don't ram their ideas down my throat. My friends can do anything they want as long as they're my friends. I don't complain about who they date or what they do.

I've got one friend who stole my pistol and shot two people because he got pissed off. I don't approve of that type of behavior, but he's still my friend. He apologized for taking my gun. He's out of prison now. I played golf with him today. I mean, he gets a little goofy around women. Women drive him over the deep end. He runs into some women who would drive me over the deep end, but they drive him completely insane. He's still my friend. I don't judge him for it. Like I say, I don't recommend people go out and do that sort of behavior. He served his time.

I know people judge me. I don't really give a shit. I don't care if people don't like me or not. I ain't going to change. Oh, I might change some, but I ain't going to change my philosophy. It might be the stupidest philosophy in the world, but it's mine. You know, consider me stupid, but it's my philosophy. [A chip off the old block?]. I don't care how smart someone is, I ain't going to start thinking the way they want me to. You find it more and more today that people forget who they are. They think too much of themselves, or go to the other extreme and think nothing of themselves. You can tell that when they drive. You've seen it. There ain't nobody behind you and this car will pull out right in front of you and drive a block and a half down the road and turn. You know, they couldn't have waited one more second? They had to get in front of you, and then they get an attitude because you're on *their* ass? Excuse me! I had two women the other day right over on Fleur Drive wanting to finger me because they pulled out right in front of me and wondered why I'm on their ass. They pulled over and yelled, "Get off our ass!" And I said, "There ain't nobody behind me, get on my ass." And they did. But I didn't pay much attention. I never looked in my rearview mirror.

What do you have to say about your mom?

Talking about my mom is about like you talking about your mom—they raised us—you know—I got my ass whipped when I was bad and rewarded when I was good. You know—she was my mom. Things she done outside, I ain't going to say it's her business, but basically it was. I mean, she provided well for us. There were times when my dad couldn't find work and she carried the load. So there ain't a whole lot I can say about her. She's my mom. Your mom and my mom may have taken different roads, they had different burdens to carry and different priorities, but they're still moms. I think mom took on the role that she wanted. I

129

think that she enjoyed getting into people's faces and spotlighting and stuff like that, and enjoyed the political turmoil, and all that shit.

Did you always know she was doing that kind of thing? Even when you were young?

Oh, yeah. She worked for the Republican Campaign Committee, then the legislature, and the State House when the Republicans got into office. She was secretary to two of the governors. Basically, she's had her foot in something like that ever since I can remember.

When you were young and in school, did you ever want to bring mom for Show and Tell?

Yeah. It was one of those type of deals. Oh, I'd never bring her, but I'd brag to my friends, "Hey, let's go see her." Especially if I got in trouble or stuff with the cops (which I did) I'd say: "Let's go talk to my mom, she works for the governor." Oh, yeah, they'd say—"She'd like that!" It was understood: "I'll whip your ass if you ever come bringing cops here." We learned early on there were limits.

Tell me the story about Tony floating down the river?

[Tony was Tim's twin. He had a cerebral hemorrhage and had to be flown to Iowa City by Life Flight helicopter for brain surgery. He died not long after. The month before this, their sister Judy died of lung cancer. Soon afterward, Judy's husband committed suicide.]

Tony and I used to go fishing every evening, and about six o'clock every day we'd have a fistfight. We'd throw each other's tackle boxes and poles in the water. Then by seven we'd made up and were trying to scrounge up enough money to buy a fishing pole replacement. Every day we'd

130

do this. One day Tony got mad—we used to push each other off the railroad trestle regularly, or try to catch trains back in those days; that was kid's stuff. One day, we decided we were going to play Tom Sawyer and we launched the barge off the 2nd Avenue boat arena. Tony got on and I knew it was dangerous. I stayed back. He was floating down the river and he's screaming: "I'm going over the dam. I'm going over the dam!" And I yelled back, "Bye. I'll tell the folks! Bye!"

It was one of those things where, well, we did some vicious things to each other. At that time we were around twelve or so. Police boats rescued him. It was one of those "not so proud moments," one of those "as soon as people leave, you're going to get an ass whipping" moments. You knew you had one coming though.

It wasn't child abuse. That's one of the things wrong with our society today. Discipline. The thing about a beating and I don't mean with belts and stuff, but we were tougher kids back then than they are today. Kids today have gotten more emotional—Oh, I don't know what it is, but kids ain't the same as we was—those were just harder times. Kids today don't fear nothing, because they're not going to be disciplined. I believe kids should be disciplined, so did my folks. You should be able to discipline your child as long as it isn't abusive. Then kids today would be more respectful.

Remember the lines waiting for a paddling at the principal's office? [Yes, I sure did.] You hoped to God you didn't get the paddle with the hole in it. I always hoped that on days like that I had my Levis on, not my dress slacks. The bottom could take only so much. They knew how to make that sucker sting. It was a different era. But I don't think that many teachers abused me. Hell, you could get your ass whipped by a neighbor if you were caught stealing rhubarb and if you went home and told, you'd get it whipped there too. Of course, we weren't very smart kids either, we'd take 22 bullets and…Remember those fifty-five gallon

131

drums you could burn trash in and stuff? Well, we'd take two shells and set them on fire and watch them explode. It was different times. The stuff that I laugh about now would be considered terrorism today. I'd be in prison.

Like when I talk about mom. If we had done wrong, we used to get dressed and she'd say: You go to your room and get a clean pair of socks and a clean pair of pants. You're going to reform school tonight."

I'd whine, "If I'm going to jail, Mom, why do I need clean underwear and socks?"

"Because I'm not going to have people thinking that I'm no good!" she'd say.

[When I asked about Judy, the answer was short and to the point.]

What was Judy like?

She was smart, pretty, and died too young.

What was your dad like?

A quiet rock. He didn't say a whole lot. I think about the only time I really saw any emotion out of him was when I got shot the last time. He took the grocery money, took a Greyhound bus and came out to see me in California. He had just enough money to buy two Snickers to eat all the way from Des Moines to California. When he got there, I'd just got done with an eighteen-hour surgery. I woke up and the doc was on one side of me and Pa was on the other side. The doctor said the operation didn't work, and they were going to have to operate again tomorrow. Later Pa told me how he got to California and I asked if he had ever flown. He said No. Well, I told him, I've got enough money for you to fly home. He said he wasn't sure if he was going to like that, but he did fly home. We had two days together. It was one of those times that I knew he was there for me. Oh, he was always there for me before, but you always wondered. This time it clicked and I knew.

When my mom came to Vietnam and saw me, it was basically a political thing. She wanted to go for her—me being there was just kind of an added bonus. It was funny when she came over there on Thanksgiving; I had to eat with her in the officer's mess. My platoon was out on patrol, but they brought me in and cleaned me up. They had Chow mein for lunch. They would have their turkey dinner that night. But the enlisted men were having their Thanksgiving meal at lunchtime. So by the time she left (I don't like turkey anyway) I got Chow mein for both meals. Well, ain't that special, I thought.

There was a young French woman who was there. She'd been captured by the gooks. She was a tiny woman and had been shot a few times. She interviewed my mom and me. Every other word out of our mouths was a four-letter word. She had a little recorder like the one you're using and click, click, she's trying to not record it. Mom was getting tired of it. Then after about five seconds of that, the French woman said, "Oh, the hell with it!" She stopped trying to edit it. It was funny. All these people were stepping and fetching for mom and I remember lighting a cigarette and smoking and someone said: "Maybe your mom won't like you smoking!" And I said: "Tough shit!" And they'd said: "Wait a minute you can't say that!" And I said: "Yes, I can, she's my mom."

How much did you see her over there?

I got to see her for about an hour and a half. It was one of those type of deals where they played it up real big. They put me in a clean uniform, gave me a new rifle so I'd look good and pretty and played it up. I didn't want her to come. For one, you can't imagine how many fights I got in over that. "Momma's coming to see you," they taunted me. You know, you tell a Marine that, now—I had to put up with this!

133

I got into probably two hundred or more fistfights over her coming with people in my own outfit alone. "Momma's coming to see you." Shit, I'd been wounded a couple of times already and that put me right with them, now I got to reestablish my territory. Yeah, I know it's part of that masculine deal, but it was real. I told her not to come. Even my dad I wouldn't have wanted to come.

The second reason is that it was not that type of battle. It was a different situation. I mean, I've never been in another war, so I don't know how to compare it to anything, but we were over there fighting for somebody, and they didn't even give a shit whether you're there or not. They'd just as soon be left alone—I mean—I'd go up in the jungle and fight, it didn't bother me too much, because I could kill anything. I probably killed more trees over there than anyone. Smokey the Bear is probably still after my ass. If it moved, I shot it. A shift in a tree—I shot it. Yeah, Smokey the Bear hates me. When I was in the jungle I didn't have to determine good or evil. That's one of the things I liked about being in the jungle rather than down in base camp. They got shot at and they never were able to shoot back. But if they shot at me in the jungle, I'd chase them down. That's one of the good things.

I went some places in the jungle that I know no human ever went—no human ever had business being out there. What was I doing out there?

I sat out in the rain for thirty days. I sat there and my hands swelled up so bad they got puffy—You know how you sit in the tub too long and your hands get puffy?—and if you try to do something with them, like try to flick a lighter, you go clear down to the bone. That hurt. You take out walking, and you can feel the bottom of your feet sliding off your foot—the skin is peeling off—it's just raw meat down there. "Oh, that hurts!" I had leaches and critters all over me. I still don't like snakes.

They had a lizard over there, one that stands on its back feet and runs, one with the hood. They get three to four feet long from the tail to the head and it makes a sound. We called it a "Fuck you lizard," cause it'd get on its back legs and it would make a sound. What'd it say? It said: "Fuck you! Fuck you!" They ran all over. I woke up one day with one of them sound asleep on my chest. I pushed him off and it made that funny sound and ran off telling me to get screwed, so I opened fire on him. Every morning you'd wake up and somebody would be shooting the hell out of something—a lizard or a snake.

Six of us went out on patrol with an eighty pound pack on our back. Anything that moved in the jungle was something that didn't have any business being there. Hell, we didn't have any business being there. You can't farm up there. So don't be using that excuse. Farmers don't carry AK 47s.

To explain what we did to someone who doesn't understand what we did, it was like this: Say, Des Moines is the Marines. Des Moines decides we're going to attack Ankeny. Okay? "Tim, we're going to send your outfit to Ames. Go up to Ames and we want you to tell us what the gooks are doing and if they start coming down toward Des Moines, stop them." That was my job. Go to Ankeny. Piss them off. Make them chase you for a while so we can reinforce people. Search and destroy. Basically, that's what we'd do.

If the Marines were here in Des Moines and were going to attack Ankeny, they would go to Ames. Sometimes they'd send us to Iowa City to make sure the Iowa City gooks were going to do anything in this direction while they were attacking in Ames.

In a long distance situation like when you're fifty or seventy-five miles away from any other Americans and you get hit by about ninety gooks, you have to run like hell. Sometimes you make it, sometimes you don't.

War doesn't make any sense. It's a good, good economic booster, but it's not good for young men—especially

135

uneducated young men. Basically, Eisenhower and Kennedy. You know, people worship Kennedy, because he got shot. I don't. I never did like Kennedy. Not so much because he was a Democrat or a Republican, but he was basically trying to get us sent to a war ever sense he was in office. People worshipped that man because he got shot. Oh, he was the best president in the world, some say. Oh, bullshit! And Nixon. He won more popular votes than any other president in our history, and yet nobody voted for him. Ask people, Did you vote for Nixon? No, I didn't vote for him. Bullshit! But, somebody did. Everybody says Kennedy was a God and Nixon was an asshole, but Nixon was probably one of our better presidents.

I don't talk to Mom much about Vietnam, or anyone else. I will tell people the surface stuff. When I try to explain to people what it's like to be scared every day you're over there, I mean, every day is a new fear. I mean, you know, when you go out with six men fifty miles from the next American, and you know nobody can get to you quick enough. The fear of being out there by yourself, alone. The power you feel; you think, they ain't going to kill me. Okay, they can wound me, but they can't kill me. Okay, they can kill me, but they can't eat me. You know, they can do what they want and then you try to pull a philosophy: Well, I'm doing it for America. Oh, shit! America don't even know where I'm at or much less care. I'm doing it for the guy next to me. Maybe I can keep him alive and he can keep me alive. But that's a small meaning. When one of your friends gets killed, and you've just been talking to him, and you've been drinking with him, and you get to know him so quickly and so well in such a short period of time, and get so close to him, that he is part of your world. I mean, when you're eighteen-years-old—I keep telling people that sanity is a thin line. I got friends on both sides. I know the way back, but I've got friends on both sides. I know I've reached that fine line. There's a point where you get so scared that you've got to snap. You either snap or you're gone. You either snap, or you don't come back at all. I laugh a lot about the experience. And that's my outlet, because nothing means something. I mean, there's no meaning—it don't mean nothing. The whole cycle of life—it's just crap. There's no meaning to it. There's no ever-after. I used to believe in a religion and a God and stuff like that, but now I have a lot of Doubting Thomas in me.

Do you think I wanted my mom to come to Vietnam, to the life I was experiencing? You can bet not.

Marine Corporal Timothy Day

Judy Day

Tony Day

13

Jackie

Don't Give Me a Job Because I'm a Woman

...all things share the same breath—the beast, the tree, the man...the air shares its spirit with all the life it supports.

~ Chief Seattle, 1854

Jackie and I had been out to lunch and we are relaxing in her apartment. The clock has just chimed and I ask more questions in a I'm-full-and-lazy kind of voice as I leaf through an album.

Was it after going to Vietnam that you began to give public talks?

When I worked for the Veterans Administration, I talked mostly about volunteerism. I have a speech I give: What would we do without volunteers—particularly hospital workers. We can't get along without volunteers. We all have a priceless bank account—we all have twenty- four hours a

140

day and how we choose to spend our hours is up to us. We can waste it away or we can make it useful. It's a bank account we all have. But I started giving talks about Vietnam shortly after coming back.

How would you respond to a woman today who would say that women shouldn't volunteer their time? They're just giving a valuable resource away?

That's up to the individual woman. If she feels like she's wasting her time in doing volunteer work, then she shouldn't do it, but if she finds some value in it, then she should. Money isn't everything. And if you want to do something useful with your life you don't have to be paid. You can get enough satisfaction just being a nice person. You don't have to be a feminist to be a nice person. There are a lot of bastards in the world, both male and female. I would have to judge a feminist who made that kind of remark on what she was doing with her life. You know, I've always said I never wanted a man to give me a job just because I was a woman. I want them to give me a job because they knew I could do it better or as well as any man. Don't give it to me because I'm a woman. Give it to me because I could do the job.

Do you ever think you got a job because you're a woman?

No, I don't think I ever did. I had to prove myself. I don't think anyone ever "gave me" anything. I think I have earned everything I got, including every gray hair on my head.

What was your connection with the Iowa Commission on the Status of Women?

141

Bob Ray and I started that. I remember when I tried to talk the women into having a booth at the State Fair. They said: "Oh, I wouldn't do that!" I told them that there is no place in the state of Iowa where you can contact that many people in a short period of time if you're trying to gain recognition (this is before we became a statutory agency). I said there's no other place on earth you can meet that many people in a ten-day span of time. I talked them into it, although they said it was beneath their dignity to be at the fair.

Jackie, I see you were invited to inaugural balls. Did you go?

Some, but not all. I've never been the kind to be impressed with people in high places. I've had some friends who just wanted to go to meet people. One friend who accompanied me would say, "Let's circulate." Hell, no." I'd sit against the wall and wait for them to come to me in a social situation. That was always my attitude.

So you were never impressed with getting invitations to such things?

Nah. Nah. But I did attend many things. A lunch at the Smithsonian, the Nixon/Agnew ball, and plenty of other things. I had certain responsibilities after all.

What did you think of Nixon, Jackie?

He was stationed in Ottumwa before he was president. I met him then. He was always very nice to me. I reported to Nixon when I came back from Vietnam. I remember he gave me a pen. And I had dinner with him—I think it was September of 1965. I think Nixon got a raw deal. Clinton was

142

impeached, but didn't resign like Nixon did over Watergate. In my opinion, Nixon was more honorable than Clinton.

14

Jackie

Tender Spirit

When you are in doubt, be still, and wait;
when doubt no longer exists for you, then go forward with
courage.
So long as mists envelop you, be still;
be still until the sunlight pours through and dispels the
mists
as it surely will.
Then act with courage.

~ Ponca Chief White Eagle, 1800s to 1914

I was in Pearl Harbor standing on a high hill with some Indians. A breeze blew. My hair swirled and pulled back from my face.

One of the Indians asked, "Have you ever been to Hawaii before?"

"Not really. Oh, I've been through twice on my way to Vietnam, but didn't spend any time here."

"Do you know anyone who has spent time here?"

I smiled, "Oh yes, my husband was stationed at Pearl Harbor in the Navy."

Just as I said that, the wind stopped, still. My eyes widened in surprise. It was the Indian's time to smile, "That was his spirit come to pay tribute," he said as he took my arm and looked off into the sea breaking over the rocks. It was Harold. I knew it. I felt it.

That afternoon in a Talking Circle Ceremony sage was lit and passed around. The rising smoke rose toward the face, cleansing each person of impurities, allowing them to say whatever was on their minds.

One woman announced that a Tepee Creeper raped her. One man confessed to being an alcoholic.

I thanked God for being amongst these people.

That evening I danced around the fire with the other Indians.

Of course, at my age all I have to do is jiggle up and down. I let the warriors do the real dancing.

Thirty years ago the Indians were living in wicki-ups along the Iowa River that flooded every spring in heavy rain. The land was very poor. The casinos have changed all that. Many people objected to the casinos coming. One thing it has accomplished for those living on the settlement is that they now have homes, cars, and receive $3,000 a month from the casino—every man/woman/child. The money is put in a trust for the children until they graduate from high school. It's been rewarding to me to see the economy change for the better.

I once went to an Indian funeral of a woman who had been inducted into the Hall of Fame for her valuable work in cultural identity issues. She insisted that the natives continue to stay on the settlement to continue to be immersed in their customs and language until the fourth grade. After that, they could go to the public schools. This policy was adopted because of that woman's efforts.

The burial site was up on a rocky hill; it was difficult to climb, but I did. Each Indian had a handful of tobacco. The corpse had a basket on her stomach. As each Indian went by

145

they dropped the tobacco in the basket and said a prayer for her safe journey into the spirit world. She, in turn, was to answer their prayer. Everyone filed past and then a man said a prayer. The grandsons nailed the coffin shut. They had cut logs and connected them by leather and she was put on them above ground. That was curious to me.

When I was in Arizona I asked the Navajos if they still buried their dead above ground; they said no, the law prohibits it. But, they said, they don't bury their dead very deep.

There is a difference between Indians living on a reservation and those on a settlement. Reservations come under federal jurisdiction. When it's a settlement, the Indians own the land, so they can bury their own way, following their customs.

Did you know I was a den mother when my boys were in the scouts?

.Many of the crafts in the books were outdated—like making cars out of spools of thread. Well, as you know, spools haven't been made from wood for some time. Also, they had ideas like making things out of orange crates. Well, oranges haven't come in crates for some time either. I had to be inventive for the scout troops.

Once I recall using baskets, which we lined so the scouts could give them to their mothers on Mother's Day. I was always attempting to come up with a new idea. The year the theme was Indian Heritage, my friend Bill Nicholas, who had a turkey farm donated over two thousand turkey feathers to make arrows with. Harold brought out a huge piling from Riverview where he worked and they carved out a totem pole. We took the totem pole to the booth at the Scouts convention at Veterans Auditorium. The boys were really proud of their creation.

"I'll never forget the time when I thought I'd been put on a hit list for the mob," Jackie said as she dipped into her cottage cheese.

"The *mob*, Jackie?" I said wide-eyed, wondering if she'd decided to pull my leg just a tad.

Jackie laughed. "Yes. It was when I was the chairman for the East Side Little League."

Here we go again.

I laughed. "Ah, come on, Jackie. The mafia and the little league?" I said in a tone that made her smile.

"I know it sounds outrageous. But the story is true. We were at a South Side meeting discussing the upcoming Little League Parade. Most of the Des Moines Little League Organization was in favor of Don Farber [Name changed to avoid concrete booties] being the parade marshal. I mean, I was livid. Don Farber? You mean, Cock-eyed Don Farber? I asked. Everyone knew that he was a member of the mafia and under investigation by the Senate's crime committee at the time. I remember I had taken a couple of men with me to the meeting."

"As bodyguards?"

Jackie winked. "I announced, I nor the East Side Little League would have nothing to do with a parade that had this man as the parade marshal. There was quite a fervor.

We left.

Shortly after this I got a call from someone who said Don Farber wanted to know what the vendetta was I had against him. I told him I didn't have a vendetta against him personally, but I have two thousand kids who look up to people and I don't think he is the proper person to be such a person. I told him that I didn't care how much money he gave to South Des Moines That didn't buy his respect. And I warned him that I better not even slip in the bathtub, because I've told so many people that Don is out to get me, and that he'd burn for it.

Later, we had a meeting out in West Des Moines. I was called a liar and a troublemaker, and was told to mind my own business. I had no right to ostracize this person just because he was under a Senate investigation. They were out to get me, no doubt about it. But then some attorney I didn't know, and who didn't know me, stood up and said, "I don't know this lady, but she's absolutely right. You know she could have had this story all over the front page of the papers, but she didn't. I agree with her."

Then another man stood and said that when he mentioned Farber's name to some friends of his, they had said they wouldn't ride in the same car if he voted for Farber. He was voted down. Later, I was appointed chairman of the National Little League Committee. The fight had raged clear to Little League National Headquarters. But I won. The man didn't lead the parade.

Some say, Jackie winks again, that I put a hex on everyone who ostracized me. Maybe I did put a "double whammy" on them.

After all, they're all dead right now, and I'm not.

She chuckled.

I grinned.

I wasn't sure what to ask next. Then I put down my fork. "Could you tell me another story about your Indian experience in Tama?"

"Sure. Here's one. On my birthday last year the Mesquaki rented a hotel room for me. When I checked in, I had a big basket of fruit, candy, and all kinds of goodies on the table. The card read: Happy Birthday from your Mesquaki friends. That is how they treat me.

Our relationship goes back over thirty years. Another time it was my niece's birthday. There was a concert for Kenny Rogers to be put on. I decided to take my niece to the concert. I happened to mention this and when we got to Tama they took me to dinner. They had seats for me right up front to watch the concert. I remember one woman asked if I was Kenny Rogers' mother.

I suppose that was the only reason she could imagine why I would get so much special treatment.

Why else?

But, it's like that with us. We've got a special relationship, I'm like part of the family, and when we can we take care of each other, like families do.

One thing about the Mesquaki—they give great recognition to their warriors who served in the armed forces. I've always been impressed with that, and whenever I could, I suggested ways the state could honor them too. More than once the governor visited the tribe, more than once a helicopter did a fly-over on Veterans Day at my suggestion. Taking care of each other, respecting each other—that's something I'm very proud of, my relationship with the Indians. I guess that's why I was flown to Pearl Harbor to help honor those who helped raise the flag at Iwo Jima.

My connection with tribe at Tama was strengthened at the time of the creation of the Vietnam Memorial because five of the names on the memorial are Indian. David Old Bear, who was tribal chief at that time and a Marine veteran of Vietnam, started inviting me to come over to pay tribute to the Gold Star Mothers, the five mothers whose sons were killed in Vietnam. I chaired the committee and met him then. That was thirty years ago. We have developed a close relationship. Each Veterans Day I go to Tama to pay tribute to the Gold Star Mothers and present them a gift. A similar gift was presented to me. The Mesquaki Indians did not know then about my Indian background. It was something I didn't emphasize. Anyway, my great grandmother was full-blooded Sioux and the Mesquaki are an offshoot of the Sac and Fox Mississippi tribes. I never explained to them that I had Indian ancestry or that that was the basis for my interest in them."

"Do they know this today?"

"Well, pretty much. I think I told you they gave me an Indian name. The Wolf Tribe adopted me. They could have just called me old lady of course, but instead they gave me an Indian name that means Old Wolf Lady—I'm proud of that. I go over there twice a month still as a rule and have an

149

opportunity to visit with them. One of the things I think endeared me to them in one respect was years ago they had asked me if I could get them a copy of that print of the flag raising at Iwo Jima. As you probably know, one of the flag raisers was an Indian, Ira Hayes. They wanted the picture to hang in the Red Earth Veterans Convention Center.

"Last year at Veterans Day at the State Fair I was on the reviewing stand and they presented me with that picture. Later, I got together a contingent of Marines and made a formal presentation of that picture to them along with a proclamation from the governor. There was a luncheon and a picture hanging ceremony. It was a special day for us all."

Later in Jackie's apartment at Luther Park, the assisted living facility where she lived, , we looked at her Mandelas, her dream catcher, her Native American figurines and dolls given to her by her children, grandchildren, and great grandchildren.

One doll, Tender Spirit, has her hand resting on Silver Wolf. This seems a fitting keepsake for a woman lovingly named "The Old Wolf Lady" by the Wolf Tribe of Iowa.

The people in Tama are called the Red Earth People. Jackie said she knew it was most important for the Indians to be aware of their environment. Their interest in land conservation helped her become more appreciative of the natural environment. Also, she admired the fact that the Indians learned the lessons of life the hard way. This made them, she thought, more attuned to things we take for granted as givens, such as beautiful sunsets, the song of a bird, life itself.

Years before, she had made a buckskin dress beading it with shells Harold brought to her from the Pacific. She wore this garment in honor of Indian ceremonies she was invited to attend. She also wore a beaded shirt and beaded necklaces. Once a Native American woman presented Jackie with a red, white, and blue beaded necklace with tiny flags beaded into it. She wore it often. That many of Jackie's

150

jewelry and clothing have been stolen (when asked, she would not say by whom) or given away, Jackie does not regret, for they will always be in her memories. Those can never be taken away.

Surrounded by her mementos, pictures of her family at various stages of life, the chirps of a bird in a cage, a squirrel playing on the railing of the balcony, and the hourly chimes of a singing clock, Jackie Day said, "Some people make a career out of being unhappy. Instead of being thankful, they find fault. The hardest thing about getting older is to condition yourself to your limitations. The body won't do what the mind says at times. That's the hardest thing about getting old, accepting those limitations. I've always said I'm lucky if my mind doesn't go—so many are suffering from the cruel disease of Alzheimer's (one area of this place is filled with these people); a very sad situation). One thing I truly enjoy are my memories.

"If I ever get bored with myself, I just think about the good times I have had and the circumstances I was in. I think you can enjoy yourself that way. I play mind games with myself. If I get feeling sorry for myself, all I have to do is look around and see there are lots of people worse off than I am. You know that saying I like to repeat works well for me, Don't let the bastards wear you down. All our adversities—we just have to step back, then go on—we just can't step back and play dead."

Jackie looked at the picture of her dead daughter. Shortly after Judy died, her husband Bill committed suicide. Then a month later Harold died. On the day of his death, Tony had a cerebral hemorrhage and had to be flown to Iowa City by Life Flight helicopter for brain surgery.

Bang. Bang. Bang. Bang. "I had my stroke a couple of years later. Everyone said I was long overdue for the stroke," Jackie said.

"The day Tony took me into the emergency room I remember thinking I was in worse shape than I was because

I thought I was seeing little people. The ER doctor was a little person." Jackie laughed.

Since jewelry is a Jackie trademark, I asked her to talk to me about the jewelry she's famous for wearing. The birdcage sat on the counter behind my head. I sat at the table. Jackie sat in an easy chair facing the sliding glass doors and small balcony. The clock chimed. Her voice was warm and gentle as she spoke.

"Well, the little engagement ring I have on is one Harold gave me when we first became engaged. The wedding ring that went with it, my son Tony when he was five years old took to kindergarten and gave it to a little classmate. When I tried to retrieve it from her, of course, no one knew what had happened to it, so I lost that.

"The wedding ring I now have Harold bought later on when he had more money. All those rings are now soldered together so I can't lose one without losing them all. That almost happened. One time I had cleaned them and wrapped them in a Kleenex to dry. I accidentally threw them in the garbage, so later when I realized what I had done I had to retrieve them from the garbage. Fortunately, I was able to do that before they were put in the dumpster. These are my favorite rings of course.

"I have a number of Indian pieces, gifts that were given to me when I would go to Tama. At one time I had over four thousand dollars of turquoise jewelry that I intended to will to my grandchildren. They were all stolen from me at the same time my beaded medallions were stolen. That was a shame. The favorites I still have (I always wear the beaded jewelry when going to Tama or any event that has an Indian connection) are costume pieces as are those with elephants on them. Elephants have always been important to me with my work with the Republican Party. I have lots and lots of costume jewelry.

"I'd rather go without my petticoat than without my earrings. I never feel dressed without earrings. And I always wear large earrings. It probably goes back to the fact my older sisters always made fun of my big ears. I've always wanted my earrings to cover up my ears. I had a squash blossom necklace valued at twelve hundred dollars that was also stolen. All to buy drugs.

"You know, I've never had pierced ears. A staunch woman of her word, Jackie adds, my sister pierced my other sister's ears, but I told her I wouldn't get mine done until I had diamond earrings to put in them. I've never had diamond earrings, so I've never had pierced ears.

"My more expensive pieces of jewelry I bought for myself. When I worked, I waited for the bus in front of Josephs Jewelry Store. Often while waiting I would go into Josephs, indulge my weakness, and buy jewelry. I suppose everyone has something they can't resist—jewelry and expensive perfume are mine.

"Harold rarely gave me jewelry. Being a carpenter, most of the gifts I got from him came from the hardware store. I had some wonderful things such as magnetic knife bars, an under-the-counter can opener, a toaster, and an under-the-counter coffee maker.

I could always count on something from the hardware store from him as a gift. Probably one of the most unusual gifts he gave me that didn't come from a hardware store was a grandmother clock (I've always loved clocks).

"One Christmas I walked into our home and sitting in the middle of the room with a big red bow attached was that clock. That was one of the nicest gifts he gave me that didn't come from the hardware store.

It's at my son Tim's home now. I gave it to him when I moved into this apartment.

"I also have watches given to me by my granddaughter and a talking clock that tells the time. I bought that for myself. The inmates of Fort Madison made the chiming clock in the living room for me when I retired from the Parole Board. I've always enjoyed the clock and often said it was smarter than me, because it doesn't chime after ten at night, nor before 6 o'clock in the morning.

"My fondness for clocks probably comes from the fact my dad use to repair clocks as a hobby. After he retired he worked on clocks, lawnmowers, and did all sorts of handyman jobs.

"For Tim's birthday on May 1st I bought him a golfer's clock. The pendulum is a golf club that swings. I had his name put on the bill of the cap and the back of the golf shirt, so he couldn't take it back. I bought it at Tama.

"There's another gift that was very special to me. It's the Hope Chest Harold sent to me from Hong Kong. He wrote that he was sending a camphor wood chest to me for a Christmas present. We weren't married yet, and I was excited, of course; although I had no idea what camphor wood meant. I thought it was probably a medicine cabinet. December came and went and no crate arrived. I lost interest. In January when the crate arrived, my dad told me there was a gift in the living room waiting for me. When he opened it, the box was upside down. 'That's the ugliest thing I've ever seen, I've never seen anything that ugly before!' I exclaimed. I didn't like it at all. But then when we turned it over we saw the most exquisitely carved box. It was and is a beautiful thing. That became my hope chest before Harold and I were married. I gave that to Tim too. His daughter Danielle has the dollhouse that Harold made. It was completely electrified, even with an elevator. My great granddaughter plays with it now. I'm thrilled they still have it. Have you ever heard that when you make something by hand part of your being remains in the piece? I believe that."

After Jackie finished, we sat together in her apartment, each of us knowing that it was time for me to begin my research and writing. We both knew our almost weekly visits were coming to an end, and it would be a sad, uncomfortable necessary parting. I had work to do.

We hugged.

I stood and walked across the carpet.

"Hey!" Jackie called as I opened the door.

I turned.

"Remember, it's all in who you want to spend your time with."

I smiled, nodded and softly closed the door, thinking what a wise woman she is.

She was referring to the answer she gave me when I originally suggested she might want to use a more published writer than me to write her biography. She said she had offers, but had refused: "It's all in who you want to spend your time with."

Being a person who values her time, I couldn't agree more.

And I was honored she chose me for the job.

Jacqueline H. Day died at home on June 23, 2002. Her remains are buried under a tree beside Harold. Their surviving son, Timothy Day, planted the tree.

Jackie and Harold

EPILOGUE

Humankind has not woven the web of life.
We are but one thread within it.
Whatever we do to the web, we do to ourselves.
All things are bound together.
All things connect.

~ Chief Seattle, 1854

So was digging into the life of Jackie Day, my aunt by marriage, worthwhile? You bet. It was more than worth spending the five years of research and interviews. I discovered so many jewels and pointers for living as I looked at Jackie's life and compared it to my own.

No, she didn't shatter the glass ceiling, but she did crack it. She didn't become governor of Iowa, or a senator, or a legislator. Unlike a woman Jackie admired, Cherokee Chief Wilma P. Mankiller, she never became chief of a Nation.

Is being the first woman public service officer for Volunteer Services for the VA such a big deal? No, for many it might not be. But how many women born in 1918 into a life of poverty with only a high school education reached this status during their lifetime? Only a handful.

Is helping to start the Iowa Commission for the Status for Women under Governor Ray such a big deal? Well, of course, for women it was. It was a landmark move that helped women to see they should take themselves seriously and helped in raising the consciousness of men and women alike. And in Iowa the Commission was begun and advertised with the panache of a woman who understood that you had to cut through the class and color lines to make the difference wide reaching. The soapbox and booth proposed by Jackie Day at the Iowa State Fair helped accomplish this goal by reaching out to the middle-class women of Iowa and offering them a chance for knowledge and change.

Jackie Day's deep roots in her past remained a strong part of her until the day she died.

Why was it significant in history that she went to Vietnam that first time? Because she couldn't afford to go, and she was a woman. She did not let those obstacles stop her from doing what she believed was right. She was the only woman who joined the fact-finding committee. She helped others see that women can make a difference in the public arena during a time that few were stepping forward. And when she returned she made her opinions and voice heard during a time when what she had to say wasn't popular. That took guts.

Was asking an African American to be Santa Claus for VA patients in Des Moines such a big deal? Doesn't seem so now, but back then in the sixties it was—just ask Dolph Pulliam—or the Iowa vets who had their stereotype of a loved icon blown out of the water by the bold move. It was, afterall, September 30th, 1962 at the University of Mississippi in Oxford when Governor Ross Barrett vowed to "stand in the doorway" to bar James Meredith as the first black student.

What makes Jackie Day's marriage to her husband so out of the ordinary? She maintained a traditional household for fifty years while in her public role continued to break down socially accepted barriers. She championed women's rights, African and Native American status, and the veterans of Vietnam. Some might claim that if Jackie Day had left her marriage to Harold Day she might have achieved more in life: for example, she could have run for public office.

Harold was not a man of ambition. He was not the type of partner who would complement a woman who might wish to achieve such a role. He most certainly did not accompany her to social gatherings that might have been to an advantage.

We all have skeletons in our closets, skeletons that deserve to remain buried. In the past decades in America, television has unleashed people's private lives on a viewing public whose thirst never seems to get quenched from swallowing the polluted water. For what purpose? Increasing the ratings—money. Haven't we learned anything yet from our history? Who cares about the fact that the repercussions are damaging to our American social fiber? Who cares that the rest of the family must live with the embarrassment and shame of having seen their worst family secrets broadcast over a TV screen? Is this the American way?

Let's hope not.

In the 1920s British author, D.H. Lawrence wrote that Americans have iron bars around their souls. Did he mean we protect ourselves from the world? If so, those words and that idea are no longer true.

Today, Americans seem to rejoice in baring all. Is this what we should be doing at the expense of our loved ones? Jackie Day did not think so. She truly believed that humans needed to deal with their pasts, but she did not agree that the pasts had to become public knowledge.

She believed "dirty laundry" needed to be carefully examined, cleaned, and put away, not hung up for all to see. How can anyone not agree that those who were the perpetrators of abuse or violence or theft should pay for their deeds? And that the victim should deal with the act with as much help as they could get and then move on to make as best a life as they were capable of doing?

However, I will add, you will not die from facing your pain, but you may die if you run away from it. And for most who suffer from childhood trauma, it takes years to fully shed the last threads of that inner aching chaos.

Were there personal details I didn't include in this biography? Oh, yes.

I do have regrets. I didn't get a chance to ask Jackie why she didn't run for office. Or maybe I had the chance and didn't take it. That happens. Or maybe, in many ways, I thought she was showing me why she didn't run. That's possible too.

The great thing about Jackie Day was that the qualities of love and dignity meant far more to her than breaking the glass ceiling. She respected her husband and children too much to drag them through the public scrutiny that political office would mean. Yes, during the years when she might have considered running, the media was more lenient (or held a blind eye) than now with "airing dirty laundry," but, still, Jackie Day protected her private life like a lioness protects her cubs. She put her family ahead of her career during a period of history when many women were being pressured to do the opposite. She said no in her own "Jackie Day" way. She was a woman ahead of her time.

Was Jackie's life all that exciting and interesting? Not really. She was a woman who was so busy doing what she had to do for her family and the world around her that her daily routine could be considered mundane and boring. But, isn't that often the way? Those who are busy accomplishing things are too busy to have exciting lives. But then, what makes an exciting life? For people like Jackie, excitement was generated every time she felt she had achieved a goal, even if the goal was as simple a thing as making another human being laugh. One can only imagine the joyous sound that came out of that war veteran in the sixties as he laid in the hospital and saw Dolph Pullium dressed as Santa Claus. The injured man was not laughing at Pullium, he was laughing with him and Jackie, enjoying the richness of a defining moment that he had never experienced before, but

160

one that would be repeated year after year at the Veterans Hospital in Des Moines. That life-changing gift was given by Jackie Day with the help of her African-American journalist friend who dared to take a chance.

Excitement for many others may mean exotic travel or fancy dinner parties or a country club existence, but these things were not the fingers that tapped Jackie's soul. What made her blood churn and made her feel charged with life itself was when she realized that she had achieved something that only she had or even (at the time) could have accomplished. This sense of social conscience was most certainly one mechanism that made Jackie Day tick.

More than once I heard Jackie refer to herself as a clown. I wondered about that. What is a clown? According to the dictionary, it is a man (I'll change that to "person," thank you, Mr. Webster) whose work is entertaining in a circus or vaudeville by antics, jokes, tricks, etc.; a jester; buffoon. The wise William Shakespeare knew that the "fool" was often the one who disguised wisdom behind those antics. This was the type of clown Jackie Day portrayed. She was a woman worth listening to—a woman full of straight shooting, multi-faceted truths. Oh, you laughed all right, but after the laughter died down, you paused—thinking about what she had said—or what had just happened. Jackie Day used her gifts to great advantage up to the day she died.

And another thing about Jackie—she wasn't merely a "talker" like she said. You know who I mean—those people who talk a lot and seem to know all the answers, but who refuse to listen when you try to throw in your opinion. Talkers are people who want or expect you to accept what they say as God's truth. Not because it is, but because they've said it. They are the ones that if you express an opposing opinion, you know that you are close to being crossed off their list of associates. It's my way or the highway. They tend to be "black" and "white" thinkers. They bristle at your words. They actually believe that there are only a few "truths" and they are trapped in concrete. They are not conversationalists. They are talkers.

Sometimes when people get to be in a position of power in the world they occupy, they turn into talkers. And sometimes, even worse, they talk about people, not ideas. Well, that was the other refreshing thing about Jackie. She loved people. Loving them meant she wanted to hear what they had to say and she didn't talk about anyone behind their back. She believed in diversity and difference of opinion and encouraged others to share their ideas with her. By doing this, she kept in touch with others, she continually learned, and, consequently, life was always charged with vitality.

Jackie style.

When someone made Jackie Day mad, she would think, This too will pass. Why? Because she knew that by allowing that person to raise her blood pressure, she was giving that person power. Native American wisdom encased Jackie's soul and was the basis for her life philosophy.

Needless to say, the mere breadth and diversity of the roles Jackie Day played with finesse, honesty, and dignity throughout her lifetime should make us all tip our multiple hats.

No doubt Jackie was a woman who thrived on challenges and diversity in her life. Until her death, she remained actively involved in society around her and lived her life to the fullest.

And my final comments: Jackie Day was tough as a stainless steel spike and smart as a leather whip's snap. She had a soul firmly wrapped in laughter, charm, and caring for her fellow humans. Now if those aren't qualities worth emulating, then what are?

In the Plaza of Heroines in front of J. Catt Hall at Iowa State University there is a brick to honor Jackie Day laid there among the thirty-two hundred other bricks.. Each brick has the name of a different Iowa woman stamped in the fired clay.

162

Bibliography

Branstad, Terry. Personal interview with the former governor. West Des Moines, Spring 2001.

Day, Timothy. Personal interview. Des Moines, IA, Winter 2001.

Heartland Technology Team. Parole Board. 9/1/2003. http://www.aea11.k12.ia.us/tech/icn/Telejustvocab.

Hullihan, Robert. "Jackie Day: Off on a New Crusade." *Des Moines Sunday Register*, pp.1, 11. Des Moines, IA, July 13, 1975.

Iowa Commission on the Status of Women. Department of Human Rights. Nelson, Charlotte. 11/18/2003. http://www.state.ia.us/government/dhr/sw/index.

Iowa Law Enforcement Academy/History. 2/29/2004, p.1. http://www.state.ia.us/government/ilea/faq_/history.

Iowa Women's Hall of Fame. Jacqueline Day. Department of Human Rights. 3/29/2004. http://www.state.ia.us/dhr/sw/iafame-day.

Park, Roy, Ph.D. Personal interview. Des Moines, IA, Winter 2001.

Pulliam, Dolph. Personal interview. Des Moines, IA. Winter 2001.

Ray, Robert. Personal interview with the former governor. Des Moines, IA. Winter 2001.

Skinner, John. Personal interview. Des Moines, IA. Spring 2001.

Women's Rights Movement. "The Path of the Women's Rights Movement, 1884–1998. 11/18/2003. http://www.legacy 98. org/timeline.

ACKNOWLEDGMENTS

Conrad and Danielle, my children and their spouses, through their love and respect encouraged my writing and research.

My partner Tom saved and continues to save me from my obsessiveness. My Florida writing colleague Sherry Koop helped me bring closure to the long process. My Iowa City writing group provided feedback, valuable editing, and constant approval. The Iowa Arts Council and Kirkwood Community College gave me their support both financially and psychologically by validating the worth of the project.

The Historic Preservation Director, Johnathan Buffalo at the Mesquaki Tribal Museum provided the Native American translation for *The Old Wolf Lady*.

Jackie's photographs, which she granted permission to use before she passed, add depth to my writer's journey and I trust, to Jackie's story.

Tim Day made sure I received the photos of his brother and sister through my brother Art. My sister Julie assisted me in locating Tim. My other siblings and in-laws continually encouraged the research.

Fine artist Peg Cullen drew the portrait of Jackie that graces the cover. When I first saw the drawing, I was amazed how she'd captured Jackie's sparkling, intelligent eyes.

To these people and organizations, and to all the others who answered with an unequivocal "yes" as this project continued and evolved, I say thank you from the depths of my heart.

ABOUT
THE
AUTHOR

jd daniels` prize-winning fiction and poetry has appeared in various publications, including: *PEN Women's Magazine, riverbabble, The Broad River Review, The Sylvan Echo, The Elkhorn Review* and *Doorknobs & BodyPaint Fantastic Flash Fiction: An Anthology.* She received a prize for poetry from Emerson College/Cambridge University, is listed in the Iowa Arts and Poets & Writers Directories and is an active member of PEN Women of Southwest Florida. Her poetry has inspired painters, clay sculptors, and dancers. *The Old Wolf Lady: A Biography, First Edition* was published in 2005 by grants from the Iowa Arts Council and Kirkwood Community College.

She was awarded her Doctor of Arts degree from Drake University for her collection of poems, *Currents That Puncture* and is co-founder and an editor of *Prairie Wolf Press Review.*

Her book of poetry *Say Yes* was published in 2013 and made the *Cedar Rapids Gazette* bestseller list. Her mystery *Through Pelican Eyes* was released in 2014. A novella, *Minute of Darkness,* will be released soon. The second in the Jessie Murphy mystery series will follow.

Besides her passion for writing, she enjoys walking, kayaking, bicycling, tennis, and talking and laughing with family and friends.

Visit her Website and say hello: www.live-from-jd.com

OTHER BOOKS
BY THE AUTHOR

Poetry

Currents that Puncture: A Dissertation
Say Yes

Fiction

Through Pelican Eyes

jd